About Cosmos

CW00508954

Cosmos is the journal of The Traditi
published annually in Edinburgh.
The annual subscription is £20 or the equivalent in other currencies
(or £15 for subscribers within the UK). Particulars about payment may
be found on the website: www.tradcos.co.uk/ or at www.facebook.com/
TradCos/
The website also carries information about back issues of the journal
and about related conferences.

Cosmos is concerned with exploring myth, religion and cosmology across
cultural and disciplinary boundaries and with increasing understanding
of world views in the past and present. We welcome all academic papers
that contribute to our better knowledge about mythology, folk beliefs and
legends, folktales, rituals, music, art and crafts etc. from all over the
world, and our better understanding of their underlying symbolic
meanings, applying any method, from comparative, structural researches
to presentations of fieldwork, research discoveries, and so on.

Papers are invited from all disciplines including, but not limited to,
ethnology, anthropology, folklore studies, history, art history, archaeology,
philology, literature, theology, medicine, psychology, musicology etc.
While papers on any part of the world's mythological issues are welcomed,
we would especially like to encourage more authors dealing with European
mythology and worldview to submit their papers. This information is
also on our website: www.tradcos.co.uk. Submissions to the journal should
be in English and will be peer reviewed. Please send your submission in
Word document, with minimal formatting:

either by email attachment to admin@tradcos.co.uk
or on a CD to Dr Louise S Milne, School of Art, Edinburgh College
of Art, University of Edinburgh, Lauriston Place, Edinburgh, EH3 9DF,
Scotland, United Kingdom.

For instructions to the author, see the inside back cover of the issue,
as well as the website.

COSMOS

THE JOURNAL OF THE TRADITIONAL COSMOLOGY SOCIETY

VOLUME 32   2016

EDITOR: LOUISE S. MILNE

EDITORIAL ASSISTANTS:
PM CICCHETTI AND SEÁN MARTIN

TYPESETTER: EVE SCOTT

CONTENTS

Cosmos **Advisory Board**

© 2016 Traditional Cosmology Society.

The Traditional Cosmology Society is a charitable body, registered in Scotland, Reg. No. SC004052

Published by Mutus Liber, BM Mutus Liber, London,WC1N 3XX.

ISSN 0269-8773

Editor's Note

We present here our final set of papers emanating from the Colloquia, Thinking About Celtic Mythology in the 21st Century, organised by Emily Lyle, held at the University of Edinburgh between 2013 and 2015.

To complement these, and develop the theme of the Colloquia, we include further materials dealing with Celtic matters. We present first the edited transcript of a session dealing with Desmond Bell's documentary film about the great Irish storyteller Seán ÓhEochaidh (1913-2002), held at the Institute of Advanced Studies, University of Edinburgh.

The bulk of the review section deals with new works in Celtic mythology, including two responses to James Mallory's study of what he calls the Irish Dreamtime. Finally, we have a special section honouring our Editor Emeritus, Emily Lyle: three responses to her important recent book *Ten Gods: A New Approach to Defining the Mythological Structures of the Indo-Europeans* (2012).

LOUISE S. MILNE

PART 1

Papers from the Colloquia, *Thinking About Celtic Mythology in the 21st Century*

Celtic & Scottish Studies, School of Literatures,
Languages and Cultures, University of Edinburgh

'Failed Birth and Rebirth': A Case Study in the Reconstruction of an Indo-European Myth

ANNA JUNE PAGÉ

ABSTRACT. *The theme of "failed birth and rebirth" was first described by Stephanie Jamison (1991) and later characterized as a narrative pattern of Indo-European origin by Angelique Gulermovich Epstein (1994). In this study I present further evidence attesting the pattern in Celtic and Greek sources, discuss some non-Indo-European comparanda, and evaluate Gulermovich Epstein's claim that the basic pattern is Indo-European.*

KEYWORDS: *Failed birth and rebirth, Indo-European mythology, Greek mythology, Celtic mythology, Cú Chulainn, Dionysus, Pryderi, blood-clot, birth from blood, miscarriage.*

INTRODUCTION

The phrase "failed birth and rebirth" is taken from Stephanie Jamison's discussion of the birth of Atri in *The Ravenous Hyenas and the Wounded Sun: Myth and Ritual in Ancient India*. It refers to a narrative pattern in which a birth fails, producing only a non-viable fetus. That fetus is then contained for a period of secondary gestation, leading to the successful rebirth of the foetus as a living child.

I begin with a review of previous studies, and then argue for the inclusion of two additional stories to the corpus of Indo-European narratives in which the pattern appears: the birth of Pryderi in *Pwyll Pendeuic Dyuet* and the birth of Cú Chulainn in *Compert Con Culainn*. I examine the especially strong parallels between the birth of Cú Chulainn and the "Orphic" accounts of the birth of Dionysus, which demonstrate the possibility of multiple cycles of failed birth and rebirth. Finally, I introduce a number of non-Indo-European comparanda and evaluate the claim that this theme is of Indo-European origin.

PREVIOUS STUDIES OF THE PATTERN

Jamison reviews various accounts of Atri's birth, including one found in the *Śatapatha Brāhmaṇa*, in which it follows a conflict between Atri's father Manas ("Mind") and his mother Vāc ("Speech") (1991, 212–3). When they appeal to Prajāpati for judgment, he judges in favour of Manas, and Vāc, who is pregnant, suffers a miscarriage. The gods then gather together, collect the miscarried foetus and place it in a container from which Atri is later born.

Other accounts of Atri's birth provide additional details to the story. In the *Vādhūla Sūtra* we are told that Vāc does not merely miscarry her child, but that her pregnancy is forcibly aborted by Manas (Jamison 1991, 221). According to the *Jaiminīya Brāhmaṇa*, Manas is also the father of Vāc's child (Jamison 1991, 244–5). A final, potentially telling detail is provided by *Rig Veda* V.78.4, where Atri is said to have called on the Aśvins for help at the moment of his birth (Jamison and Brereton 2014).

The story of Atri's birth provides us with the basic narrative framework for stories about failed birth and rebirth: first, the failure (Vāc's miscarriage); then the fetus is placed into a container; finally, the newborn emerges from the same container in a second, successful birth. The story of Atri's birth is only one instance of a fairly common type of miraculous birth in Indian mythology, attested both during the Vedic period and later, with multiple occurrences in the *Mahābhārata* (Jamison 1991, 239).

Building on Jamison's work, Angelique Gulermovich Epstein (1994) identifies further examples of the pattern in Greek and Welsh stories, suggesting that the pattern might originally be Indo-European. First, she discusses the birth of Lleu Llaw Gyffes in *Math uab Mathonwy*, the "Fourth Branch" of the *Mabinogi*. Math asks his niece Aranrhod to step over his magic wand as a test of her virginity, but when she does she gives birth to a child. Aranrhod flees, but leaves behind what the text describes as *y ryw bethan* "some little thing" (Williams 1964, 77).[1] Aranrhod's brother Gwydion seizes the thing, wraps it in a cloth – described as a *llen o bali* "a sheet of silk brocade" – and hides it in a chest. After some time, Gwydion hears a cry coming from the chest: when he opens it, he discovers the boy who will later be named Lleu Llaw Gyffes. Here again we find the core elements of the narrative pattern described above: Lleu's initial emergence from his mother's womb as "some little thing" rather than as a fully formed child (birth failure), Gwydion's subsequent capture, which confines the fetus to a chest where it continues to gestate (containment phase), until he finally emerges as a boy and is thus successfully born (re-birth).

Gulermovich Epstein compares this story with others from medieval Welsh literature, as well as further material from Indian and Greek sources, including the birth of Mārtāṇḍa/Vivasvant from Indian myth,[2] and the births of Dionysus and Erichthonius from Greek myth. In particular, the additional Welsh parallels Gulermovich Epstein traces are the story of Gwion Bach's rebirth as the poet Taliesin, as recounted in *Ystoria Taliesin*, and the story of the transformation and imprisonment of two fighting dragons in *Cyfranc Lludd a Llefelys*. Based on her analysis of these stories, she formulates the following narrative pattern, consisting of four principal episodes: first, a miscarriage or other form of failed birth produces "a type of reproductive material without human form." Second, a man places it in a container. Gulermovich Epstein notes a great deal of variation in the types of containers used, as well as episodes of double containment. Third, the "thing" gestates in the container and then emerges. Fourth, the "thing" is transformed (1994, 156–7).

Independently of the work of Jamison and Gulermovich Epstein, Leslie Ellen Jones (2005) also identifies a similar narrative pattern, or "bundle of motifs." Jones begins with a discussion of the story of Lleu's birth, although her interest in the story begins with Lleu's containment in the chest rather than with his first appearance as an unformed "little thing." She compares Lleu's birth with other tales of boys found in boxes, or otherwise contained or imprisoned, and identifies the following motifs as consistently present in some form or another in a variety of mythological sources, and especially manifest in the story of Lleu's birth:

> The incubation in a box, the problems with a name, the announcement that the boy is "done" through an unusual sound, the boy's association with birds and with theriomorphism, his abandonment by his mother and adoption by an older man, and his generally non-martial character. (Jones 2005, 224)

Of particular interest here are the items "incubation in a box" and "abandonment by the mother and adoption by an older man," the latter corresponding to the man who puts the "thing" into incubation in Gulermovich Epstein's formulation of the pattern.

THE BIRTH OF PRYDERI

Pwyll Pendeuic Dyuet, the "First Branch" of the *Mabinogi*, is composed of three principal episodes. The third episode focuses on the birth of Pryderi to Pwyll and Rhiannon, a woman from the Otherworld. After their marriage fails to produce children for several years, Pwyll's men encourage him to find a new wife. Pwyll decides to wait another year, and during that time Rhiannon becomes pregnant with a son. Though Pryderi's birth is central to the plot of *Pwyll Pendeuic Dyuet*, few details about it are provided. We are told only that it happens during the night and that the child vanishes immediately after birth. The women charged with watching over Rhiannon fear that they will be blamed for his disappearance, and so they fake his death and incriminate her for his murder by smearing her face with the blood of dead puppies, and by spreading their bones in front of her. The blood on Rhiannon's face leads people to believe that she has not only killed her son, but also eaten him, and thus Pryderi is believed to be dead both by his parents and by everyone else. Within the narrative, the perceived reality is that he has been destroyed by his own mother. Pryderi's disappearance thus has the same effect as a miscarriage or failed birth, in that Rhiannon's pregnancy fails to produce a living child.

Pryderi's subsequent reappearance is described in greater detail than his birth. On the eve of May-day, Teyrnon is standing guard over a mare who gives birth to a foal on that same night each year, only to have the foal disappear. In order to discover the cause of the missing foals, Teyrnon waits with the mare. A creature comes and attempts to take the foal, but Teyrnon cuts off its arm. The creature flees: Teyrnon pursues it, but fails to catch it. When he returns to his home, Teyrnon finds a baby on his doorstep, and in time he realizes that this is Rhiannon's missing child. It is clear, though not explicitly stated, that the creature that had been stealing the foals had also taken Pryderi, and had been forced to abandon him after Teyrnon's attack. We are left to assume that the separate events of Pryderi's birth and disappearance and his reappearance on Teyrnon's doorstep take place on the same night, that is, on the eve of May-day, and that Pryderi's birth co-occurs with that of the foal.

Pryderi's re-emergence into the world at this point is as a child with no origin. When he is adopted and named by Teyrnon, he is given a new identity and thus a second birth or rebirth. As in the Vedic story of Atri's birth, we find that rebirth requires some assistance. Whereas in Atri's case this assistance was provided by the Aśvins, the twin gods associated with horses, here we have Teyrnon rescuing Pryderi while attempting to rescue a horse. Pryderi is both twinned with a foal and, functionally and symbolically, a foal himself. His mother, Rhiannon, is associated with Epona, the Horse-Goddess known from Continental Celtic sources.[3] When Rhiannon first appears in the narrative, she is riding a supernatural horse, and her punishment for killing her son is to wait by the mounting block at the gate of the court each day for seven years and to carry any who ask on her back, performing the role of a horse. Pryderi is thus the son of a horse and he is stolen by a creature that before this had only been known to take foals from a mare, rendering her functionally barren, since, like Rhiannon, she cannot successfully produce offspring. In seeking to correct the barrenness of the mare by rescuing her foal, Teyrnon also corrects Rhiannon's apparent barrenness by rescuing her child.

Pryderi's abduction and apparent death provide the "failed birth" stage of the pattern, and his rediscovery and adoption by Teyrnon serve as his rebirth. The intervening period can be treated as the time during which he is contained. Containment functions as a period of absence during which a child who has entered the world too soon is removed from it until a more appropriate or auspicious moment. In Pryderi's case, he is absent from the narrative – and apparently dead – between the time of his disappearance and the moment of his reappearance on Teyrnon's doorstep.

A further detail of Pryderi's reappearance offers a form of physical containment, and suggests another connection with the Welsh stories treated in Gulermovich Epstein's study: when Teyrnon discovers Pryderi on his doorstep, he is described as being wrapped in a *llenn o bali* (Williams 1964, 22). As previously noted, a *llen o bali* was used to wrap both Lleu's first form as a "little thing," and one is also used to enclose the two fighting dragons in *Cyfranc Lludd a Llefelys*, who, subsequent to a series of transformations, were wrapped in the cloth and then also placed into a chest and buried. The dragons were contained thus because they had caused an "oppression" (*gormes*) in Britain. This "oppression" is the scream of one of the dragons, heard on the eve of May-day each year – precisely when the events surrounding Pryderi's birth and the yearly disappearance of the foals take place. Although Gulermovich Epstein does not call attention to the fact, the dragons are also strongly associated with miscarriage and barrenness: among the effects of the dragon's cry are that *y collei ... [y]r gwraged eu beichogyeu* "women miscarried" and animals, the woods, the fields, and the waters were left barren (Roberts 1975, ll.35–41).

In addition to the features of failed birth, containment, rebirth, and adoption by a man, which are all present in the narrative patterns described by Gulermovich Epstein, Jones' bundle of motifs offers, several additional points of correspondence. When Teyrnon adopts Pryderi he names him Gwri Wallt Euryn, but when his true parentage is established and he is reunited with Rhiannon, she declares that his return has freed her from her *pryder* "anxiety," and so he is renamed Pryderi, reflecting the problems regarding the boy's name to which Jones refers.

We also find that the re-emergence of the child is signalled by what Jones describes as an "unusual sound." In this case, the appearance of the creature that has come to steal Teyrnon's foal is accompanied by *twrwf mawr* "a great commotion," and later *twrwf a diskyr* "a roar and a wail together" (Williams 1964, 22). Furthermore, Jones comments that the boys of her study are frequently associated with "birds and theriomorphism" (2005, 224). Although Pryderi is not associated with birds, he is associated with animals – with dogs, through the physical substitution of puppies for his missing body after his failed birth – and even more firmly with horses, as seen above.

The story of Pryderi's birth thus contains many of the features associated with the pattern of failed birth and rebirth, as well as several of those included in Jones' bundle of motifs, and it should be set alongside the birth of Lleu, the reincarnation of Gwion Bach as Taliesin, and the containment of the dragons in *Cyfranc Lludd a Llefelys* as a Welsh attestation of this narrative pattern.

THE BIRTH OF CÚ CHULAINN

The story of the conception and birth of Cú Chulainn (*Compert Con Culainn*) exists in two variants. I refer here only to the earlier one, which dates to the 8th or 9th century.[4] Already Gulermovich Epstein suggests (but does not pursue) the possibility that Cú Chulainn's birth might be connected to the other stories she analyses. Her suggestion is based on the fact that in *Compert Con Culainn* three attempts are required before Cú Chulainn is successfully born. Kim McCone's discussion of Cú Chulainn's birth schematises it as occurring over three separate stages:

> Cú Chulainn's fully supernatural origin in stage one is mediated by stage two, comprising an annunciation and the non-sexual impregnation of a virgin human mother by the supernatural father, into the fully human stage three.[5] (1990, 199)

In the context of the narrative pattern under consideration here, we can read this as two failed births preceding a final successful birth.

First, we have what McCone calls the "fully supernatural" birth: Cú Chulainn is born to divine parents, described here as *lánamain*, a married couple (van Hamel 1978, §3). While his mother is never named, his father is later revealed to be Lug mac Ethnenn, of the Túatha Dé Danann.[6]

The birth takes place in a mysterious house that the Ulstermen find while seeking shelter during a snowstorm in the middle of the night. Crucially, Cú Chulainn's birth happens at the same time as two twin foals are born to a mare standing in the doorway of the house. As in the story of Lleu's birth, then this story features the birth of twins, and, as in the story of Pryderi's birth, the hero's birth takes place simultaneously with the birth of horses which will later belong to him.[7] Moreover, as with the birth of Atri, twin horses are present: in the flesh here, as they are born, and symbolically in the Vedic story, in the form of the Aśvins.

The Ulstermen take the child and give him to Deichtine to raise, but he dies: this first birth is therefore failed. The second stage of Cú Chulainn's birth begins when Deichtine attempts to drink water, but, each time she takes a sip, a little insect jumps toward her mouth. As I discuss below, a woman conceiving a child by swallowing a small insect in water is a motif found in several other medieval Irish stories. That same night, Lug visits Deichtine in a dream and informs her that she is bearing his child, and that this is the same child who had previously been in her care and had died. When it becomes clear that Deichtine is pregnant and that there is no known father, she is offered in marriage to Súaltaim mac Róich. Deichtine, not wishing to go to her new husband already pregnant, aborts the semi-divine foetus and thus brings about a second failed birth.[8] Deichtine then conceives again, this time with Súaltaim as the father, and Cú Chulainn is finally born successfully.

There is no overt period of time during which Cú Chulainn is contained in this story, but we can read the second, aborted pregnancy as a form of containment. There are several other stories in which a foetus undergoes a failed birth and is then re-contained within the body of a parent, rather than in an object such as a chest. In the story of Dionysus' birth, for example, his mother Semele dies while pregnant, and her unborn child is removed from her body and transferred to Zeus' thigh, where he continues to gestate and from which he is later born. A second example from Greek myth is the swallowing of five of the Olympian gods by their father Kronos, who later vomits them up. There is also a secondary containment motif in Rhiannon's "eating" of her child in the story of Pryderi's birth.

In the story of Cú Chulainn's birth we find two episodes of failed birth, rather than the more common single episode, before a successful birth occurs, creating a total of three cycles of conception and gestation. We also find two separate mothers (Lug's unnamed consort and Deichtine) and two separate fathers (Lug and Súaltaim). The story of Gwion Bach's reincarnation as Taliesin can also be read as involving a similar triple cycle. *Ystoria Taliesin*, "The Story of Taliesin" describes how the boy Gwion Bach accidentally steals a magical potion from the witch Ceridwen. After the theft, Ceridwen pursues Gwion Bach, and both transform several times, until finally Ceridwen takes the shape of a hen and swallows Gwion Bach in the form of a grain of wheat. She thus becomes pregnant, but, when she gives birth, she cannot bring herself to kill the child. Instead, she places him inside a *korwgyl ne vol kroen* (Ford 1992, l. 87), "a coracle or a skin bag," and sets it adrift. As Gulermovich Epstein observes, the dual meaning of *bol* as "bag" but also "womb" is an overt indicator of the function of the container, which remains adrift for forty years until it is found by Elphin, who cuts it open and finds the child inside (1994, 158). He remarks upon his "radiant forehead" – *tal iesin* – and Gwion Bach is reborn as Taliesin (Ford 1992, l.141).

Strictly speaking, no miscarriage or abortion takes place in this story. We have instead a child who dies when swallowed – or at least ceases to exist as his current self – is then reborn and put into a container, and is finally reborn again as Taliesin when he re-emerges. In the Orphic version of the birth of Dionysus, we find a third example of a triple cycle of failed birth and rebirth.

THE BIRTH OF DIONYSUS

The story of Dionysus' birth is among those examined in Gulermovich Epstein's study, and Dionysus is strongly connected to cycles of birth, death, and rebirth due to his association with mystery cults and their rituals. This is especially clear in the context of ritual initiations, which are often conceived of and even enacted as a form of death and rebirth. Dionysus is called διμήτωρ "twice-born," a compound of the Greek words for "two" and "mother," thus "having two mothers" by Diodorus Siculus (Oldfather [1935] 2006, 3.62.5 and 4.4.5), which illustrates how integral his death and rebirth are to his function in Greek mythology as god of reincarnation, as well as of the vine and of madness.[9]

In the Orphic hymn to Dionysus (Hymn 30), however, he is referred to as τρίγονον "thrice-born." The second line of the hymn describes Dionysus as πρωτόγονον, διφυῆ, τρίγονον "first-born, dual-natured, thrice-born" (Athanassakis 1977, 24). The triplicity here is highlighted by the "one-, two-, three-" of the line: πρωτο-, δι-, τρί-. The hymn also refers to Dionysus δικέρωτα "two-horned" and δίμορφον "two-shaped" (a descriptor also used by Diodorus Siculus), further emphasizing his inherent multiplicity.

There are several competing traditions about Dionysus' birth, and Diodorus Siculus provides an extensive discussion of these. That most commonly known variant, and the one which forms the basis of Gulermovich Epstein's examination, identifies Dionysus as the son of Semele and Zeus. When Semele asks Zeus to appear to her as he does to Hera, he complies and appears in his chariot, accompanied by thunder and lightning, and casts a thunderbolt. Overwhelmed by the divine spectacle, Semele dies of fright, and so Zeus rescues Dionysus – described by Apollodorus at this stage as ἑξαμηνιαῖον τὸ βρέφος ἐξαμβλωθὲν (Wagner 1965, 3.4.3), "a six-month miscarried foetus" – from the fire that consumes his mother's body and sews him up in his own thigh, which acts as the container in which Dionysus undergoes his second period of gestation. At the appropriate time, Zeus removes the stitches in his thigh and Dionysus is reborn.

The Orphic tradition about Dionysus' birth makes him the son of Zeus and Persephone, rather than Semele, and thus fully divine. Details about the Orphic account of the birth of Dionysus are furnished by some of the earlier "Orphic Theogonies." My discussion of these texts relies primarily on M. L. West's *The Orphic Poems*.[10] These texts tell us that after his birth to Persephone, Dionysus was so favoured by Zeus that the jealous Titans tore him to pieces. Athena was able to preserve his still-beating heart, which she placed into a casket. Dionysus was later reborn from this heart, though explanations of the exact mechanism of this rebirth differ. One version of the story, and that which West identifies as most likely to be the true Orphic tradition, is that Zeus placed the heart in an image of Dionysus made from wood, which then came alive (1983, 162–3). Here we have not one, but two containers, and the child is reborn not *out of* the second container, but rather *as* the container, since the latter provides the physical material for his new body.

West argues that the story of Dionysus' birth, death, and rebirth is best understood "in terms of two models: initiation rituals and animal sacrifice" (1983, 140). He argues that Dionysus' dismemberment and rebirth reflect ritual initiation practices that involve the symbolic death and rebirth of the initiand, who is often "captured, taken away, and killed by a divine ancestral spirit or spirits, whose part is played by men disguised in unearthly fashion" (1983, 143). West likens these disguised men to the Titans, who used gypsum to whiten their faces and then lured Dionysus away in order to destroy him.

Interestingly, West also notes that the supernatural being (or beings) is given a terrible voice through the use of a bullroarer. We return here to Jones' discussion of the "boys in boxes" pattern as attested in Welsh literature, and more specifically to the detail concerning some sort of sound frequently accompanying the rebirth or re-emergence of the boys (2005, 224). I have previously discussed the cries that feature in the accounts of the births of Lleu and Pryderi, and the cry of the dragon in *Cyfranc Lludd a Llefelys*. These cries, like the sound of the bullroarer during initiation rituals, accompany the passage of the individual from one stage of life to another. In these rituals, the individual is destroyed before being recreated as a member of the society into which he is being integrated. The stories of failed birth and rebirth show this same cycle of destruction followed by recreation as something new, something better, and something stronger.

DIONYSUS AND CÚ CHULAINN

The competing tradition that saw Persephone as Dionysus' mother survived outside of the Orphic sources in various other accounts of his origins, including that of Diodorus Siculus, where it is presented as a separate tradition. Hyginus' *Fabula* 167 (Rose 1933) offers instead a version of the story in which the two competing traditions are reconciled, and in doing so provides a strong narrative parallel for the story of Cú Chulainn's birth. According to Hyginus, Dionysus was first born fully divine as the child of Zeus and Persephone. After his destruction at the hands of the Titans, Athena rescued his heart, which was then ground up and given to Semele to drink, and in this way she became pregnant. Later, after Semele was struck by lightning and died, Zeus took Dionysus from her womb and gave him to Nysus to care for. As we have already seen, other sources, such as the *Library* of Apollodorus, tell us that, after the fetus was rescued from Semele's body, it was sewn up inside Zeus' thigh, and from there it was later reborn. Timothy Gantz notes that "a fifth-century Red-Figure lekythos by the Alkimachos Painter ... actually shows the god emerging from his father's thigh" (1993, 112), and that, although the very early literary sources about Dionysus' birth do not mention its exact nature, the Homeric Hymn to Dionysus does refer to Zeus giving birth to him. Thus, we can be assured that Dionysus' birth as taking place from Zeus' body in some way is one of the oldest features of this myth. Here, as in the story of Cú Chulainn's birth, we have two separate mothers (one divine and one mortal), a divine father, two failed births before a successful third birth, with the second conception brought about by the mortal mother drinking something.

The motif of conception through drinking in these instances is strongly associated with reincarnation. Dionysus himself provides the physical "seed" for his conception in the form of the remains of his heart. While Cú Chulainn's second conception does not involve any physical remnant of his first birth, it is nonetheless clearly a case of reincarnation. Elsewhere in medieval Irish literature, where conception caused by drinking a small insect in water is associated with reincarnation, the insect involved is explicitly identified as a form of the being about to be conceived, and thus reincarnated. In *Tochmarc Étaíne*, "The Wooing of Étaín," the jealous Fúamnach transforms Étaín into a pool of water, which dries up and becomes a worm, which then becomes a fly. This fly eventually falls into a cup of water and is swallowed by the wife of Étar, who gives birth to a daughter called Étaín (Bergin and Best 1938, §21). In this story, we find Étaín reborn after a cycle of transformations leading up to a form of her being swallowed, thus triggering her final conception. A similar cycle can be found in *De chophur in Da Muccida* "Concerning the Quarrel of the Two Swineherds" (Roider 1979). The two swineherds are caught up in a cycle of repeated transformations, culminating in their reincarnation as the two bulls at the centre of the conflict in *Táin Bó Cúailnge*. Their rebirth comes about when, as worms in different rivers, they are swallowed by two cows who consequently become pregnant. A similar pattern, with a sequence of transformations followed by conception through swallowing, and the rebirth of the one swallowed, is found also in the story of Gwion Bach's reincarnation as Taliesin.[11]

What transpires from these stories - Cú Chulainn's, and Dionysus' and Taliesin's – is an expanded version of the same pattern previously identified in the birth tales of Atri, Lleu, Pryderi. Instead of a single cycle of failed birth followed by a successful rebirth, here multiple cycles of transformation must occur before the final birth.

NON-INDO-EUROPEAN COMPARANDA

I turn now to a selection of stories from outside the Indo-European cultural sphere that show correspondences to the stories already examined. It must be noted that this is far from an exhaustive survey of the available material, and is intended only to illustrate that this narrative pattern is present in multiple cultural contexts.

In North American mythology we find the story of "Blood-Clot Boy" (Thompson 1929, 108–13).[12] One day, while out foraging for food, an old man finds a clot of blood and brings it home for his wife to make blood-soup. The blood-clot is placed into a pot, which is covered and left over the fire to cook. After some time, a cry is heard from the pot and when the couple looks inside they find a child. In this story, the origin of the clot of blood is never explained, but in all other ways the story presents a remarkable correspondence to those found in the Indo-European context. The connection between blood, life, birth, and creation is strong for obvious reasons, and stories making use of this connection are fairly common. We find this not only in the origin stories of heroes, but also in stories about the creation of mankind. In a creation myth from the Admiralty Islands,[13] Hi-asa cuts her finger and collects the blood in a mussel-shell. She covers the shell and sets it aside, and after eleven days she opens it again and finds that the shell now contains two eggs. She covers the eggs, and, after several days, the first man and the first woman hatch from them (Dixon 1916, 109). Dixon reports a similar story in the Chatham Islands, which tells how "man originated miraculously from a clot of blood placed by two deities in a hollow tree" (1916, 62).[14] These are only two examples from a fairly extensive set of stories from Polynesia and Melanesia that feature birth or creation from blood. In these cases, however, the source of the blood is not explicitly identified as female reproductive tissue, as it is in the Indo-European stories.

Elsewhere we do find stories in which menstrual blood or miscarried fetal tissue is transformed into a child. In Tinguian[15] folklore, the *alan* spirits are known for taking women's menstrual blood or afterbirth, or even the result of a miscarriage, which they are able to transform into children. They raise these children in splendid but otherworldly surroundings, and when the identity of the children is discovered they are returned to their true parents, bringing with them riches from the houses of the spirits (Cole 1915, 15). The mechanism by which the transformation takes place is not explained in these stories, however, and thus we lack the element of containment in a secondary womb that we have seen elsewhere.

In Zulu folklore we find a closer correspondence for the Indo-European stories. There are multiple versions of the story, but the central narrative is about a young woman who is barren and who laments her childless state. Pigeons come to her and offer her assistance. They instruct her to place a clot of her menstrual blood into a pot and to close the pot tightly with clay. She must then set it aside for eight months, and in the ninth she must uncover the pot. When she does, she finds a child inside (Callaway 1868, 72–3).[16]

The correspondences between a subset of these stories has been remarked upon previously, and explanations for these similarities have been sought. In her study of the Tinguian folktales, Fay-Cooper Cole comments that:

> Previous writers ... have sought to account for certain resemblances
> in culture between Malaysia, Polynesia, and America, by historical
> connection. A part of our material – such as that of the blood-clot
> child [etc.] – may seem to lend support to such a theory. These
> similarities are assuredly suggestive and interesting, but it appears
> to the writer that the material is too scanty and the folklore of
> intervening lands too little known to justify us in considering
> them as convincing proof of borrowing over such immense
> distances. (Cole 1915, 30)

Cole does not seem to have been aware of the African or Indo-European
comparanda, but they would likely have increased her sense that a singular
origin for the narrative pattern followed by extensive borrowing is a
highly unlikely scenario.

CONCLUSION

Gulermovich Epstein concludes her study by acknowledging that she has
simply "proclaimed" the pattern as Indo-European (1994, 159). This claim
rests largely on the undeniable similarity of the essential narrative structure
shared by the Indo-European stories. Since the intent of her article is not
to argue for an Indo-European origin or to reconstruct a Proto-Indo-
European original, but rather to gain insight into the stories through
comparison, she does not engage with what it means to label the pattern
"Indo-European." The relationship between the Indo-European stories
must be examined more carefully, however, particularly in light of the
non-Indo-European comparanda that I have presented.

In linguistics, the label "Indo-European" makes a clear claim that the
item in question is directly inherited from a Proto-Indo-European original.
Frequently, this claim is implicit when a cultural feature, such a myth,
is labelled as Indo-European, and this introduces the possibility of
reconstructing an original proto-type. This is in fact a requirement in
linguistics: if one cannot reconstruct a Proto-Indo-European form of the
feature in question (whether a phoneme, lexeme, morpheme, etc.), then
such feature cannot be securely claimed as Indo-European. In dealing
with myth, however, we must acknowledge a different theoretical

framework and a different set of assumptions than those used in linguistics. Enrico Campanile (1990, 11) has argued that, in reconstructing aspects of culture, we should concern ourselves only with understanding what is potentially Indo-European, not with what is uniquely Indo-European. M. L. West has made the argument even more forcefully, stating that his object "is to identify whatever is Indo-European, not just what is distinctively or exclusively Indo-European" (2007, 20) and that the reconstructive method cannot be:

> invalidated by objections on the lines 'the parallel motifs that you note in this and that source need not imply a common Indo-European prototype, because they occur all over the world'. If a motif is indeed universal, all the more likely that it was also Indo-European. (2007, 21)

To return to our specific group of stories: the very fact that narratives about attempts to correct or resolve reproductive failures are so wide-spread suggests that, as in so many other cultures, the speakers of Proto-Indo-European – regardless of their unity as a cultural group – would have had stories of this type. This claim does not require the additional claim that each of the Indo-European versions is directly inherited from a single prototype.

Indeed, the wide-spread attestation of this narrative type can be explained in two ways. The first is monogenesis, with large diffusion through inheritance and extensive borrowing, while the second is polygenesis, with transmission via more limited inheritance and borrowing. Polygenesis is most likely, given that the experience of childbirth is universal, as are the problems associated with it. It is unsurprising that stories about attempts to repair the effects of some of these problems are widespread, and that they employ the same strategies – an imitation of natural gestation in a secondary vessel – in order to do so.

That said, the Indo-European sources include certain details that are not present elsewhere, such as the presence of horses. Those details bear further investigation, and allow for the possibility that the Indo-European stories might share a single source, either through inheritance or borrowing. More suggestively, it is only in the Indo-European sources that we have what I consider to be the core three elements of the pattern: failed birth, secondary gestation of the result of failed birth in a container, and rebirth. The North American, African, Polynesian, and Micronesian comparanda lack the initial element of failed birth, while the Tinguian allows the possibility of failed birth but lacks the element of containment. While further study of the pattern in both Indo-European and other contexts is certainly called for, it is thus very likely that the theme of "failed birth and rebirth" was part of the narrative tradition of the Proto-Indo-European speakers. The association between the narrative theme, the belief in various forms of reincarnation, and the practice of ritual initiation, also requires further study and should provide additional insights into the development and distribution of these stories.

Anna June Pagé is a lecturer in the Institut für Sprachwissenschaft at the University of Vienna, Austria. annajune.page@gmail.com

Note: This article is based in part on the third chapter of my dissertation "Birth Narratives in Indo-European Mythology" (Pagé 2014). Earlier versions of some of this material were presented at the meeting of the Celtic Studies Association of North America at the University of Toronto (2012) and at the colloquium "Thinking About Celtic Mythology in the 21st Century" at the University of Edinburgh (2015). I am grateful to the members of my dissertation committee and to the participants of both conferences for their comments.

Notes

1 All translations are my own unless otherwise indicated.

2 Gulermovich Epstein relied on Jamison for her discussion of the Indian texts. See further Jamison 1991, 204–8.

3 On this point see further Ford 1977, 4–12 on the "Adventure of the Mare and Boy" in Celtic myth, and Hemming 1998.

4 See Thurneysen 1921, 268–73 for discussion of the two versions of this story.

5 Ó Cathasaigh 1985 has also discussed the ways in which the hero mediates between the gods and humanity, with specific reference to Cú Chulainn and the story of his birth.

6 It should be noted that Lug is the Irish cognate for the Welsh Lleu. On linguistic and other correspondences between the Welsh Lleu, the Irish Lug, and the Gaulish Lugus, see Mac Cana, *Celtic Mythology*, pp. 27–9.

7   Although there are no horses present in connection with Lleu's birth, he
     is associated with horses later in his life. The Fourth Branch states that,
     when grown, he was capable of riding any horse: *[g]allwys marchogaeth
     pob march*, literally "he was capable of the horsemanship of every horse"
     (Williams 1964, 22). He is also known in the Welsh Triads as the owner
     of one of the "three bestowed horses of the Isle of Britain" (Triad 38),
     which is listed as *Melyngan Mangre, march Lleu Llaw Gyffes* "Pale
     Yellow of the Stud, horse of Lleu Skilful-Hand" (trans. Bromwich 1961,
     97).

8   Bondarenko 2014 discusses the story of Cú Chulainn's birth in his study
     of reincarnation in Irish literature. He notes other interpretations of this
     episode, including one according to which Cú Chulainn is a reincarnation
     or avatar of Lug himself.

9   Additional attestations of διμήτωρ, as well as the related form διμήτριος,
     in reference to Dionysus, are listed in Liddell and Scott's *Greek-English
     Lexicon*.

10   For further discussion of the Orphic myths of Dionysus, see Bernabé
     2002 and Johnston 2013.

11   For discussion of this motif in connection with metempsychosis and
     reincarnation, see Bondarenko 2014. The motif is also found without the
     association with reincarnation in accounts of the births of Conchobar and
     Conall Cernach. See Pagé 2014, 111–3 and 136–9 for discussion of this
     motif in Irish sources, and 159–63 for a partial Indian parallel. It should
     be noted that the motif is not exclusively Celtic, or even Indo-European.
     A story about the creation of mankind recorded on the Caroline Islands
     in Micronesia describes how Ligoapup, daughter of the creator Luk,
     "drank some water which had been collected in the hollow of a tree.
     Without knowing it, with the water she swallowed a tiny animal, and
     made fruitful by this, she bore a girl-child" (Dixon 1916, 251).

12   Thompson reports versions of this story from most areas of the continental
     United States, as well as southern Canada. The most detailed study of the
     Blood-clot Boy stories is that of Gerow 1950. See especially pages 4–15
     for a discussion of the tale-type and its distribution.

13   The Admiralty Islands are currently a province of Papua New Guinea.

The inhabitants of the Islands predominantly speak languages belonging to the Oceanic branch of the Austronesian family, but there are additionally some languages that are as yet unclassiied.

14   The Chatham Islands are located to 650 kilometers to the east of New Zealand and are primarily inhabited by Māori and Moriori, descendants of a much earlier wave of Māori settlers.

15   The Tinguian, also known as the Itnag, are an Austronesian ethnic group from the Philippines.

16   When the folktales translated and published by Callaway were collected, the Zulu Kingdom was an independent monarchy covering much of modern South Africa, and particularly the province of KwaZulu-Natal.

References

Athanassakis, Apostolos N., ed. and trans. 1977. *The Orphic Hymns*. Missoula, MT: Scholars Press for The Society of Biblical Literature.

Bergin, Osborn and R. I. Best, ed. and trans. 1938. "Tochmarc Étaíne." *Ériu* 12:137–96.

Bernabé, Alberto. 2002. "La toile de Pénélope: a-t-il existé un mythe orphique sur Dionysos et les Titans?" *Revue de l'histoire des religions* 219 (4): 401–33.

Bondarenko, Grigory. 2014. "The Migration of the Soul in Early Irish Tales." In *Studies in Irish Mythology*. Berlin: Curach Bhán Publications.

Bromwich, Rachel, ed. and trans. 1961. *Trioedd Ynys Prydein. The Welsh Triads*. Cardiff: University of Wales Press.

Callaway, The Rev. Canon, ed. and trans. 1868. *Nursery Tales, Traditions, and Histories of the Zulus, in their own words, with a translation into English, and notes*. London: Springvale, Natal and Trübner and Company.

Campanile, Enrico. 1990. *La ricostruzione della cultura indoeuropea*. Pisa: Giardini.

Cole, Fay-Cooper. 1915. *Traditions of the Tinguian: A Study in Philippine Folk-Lore*. Chicago: Field Museum of Natural History.

Dixon, Roland B. 1916. *The Mythology of All Races. Volume 9: Oceanic*. Boston: Marshall Jones Company.

Ford, Patrick K., trans. 1977. *The Mabinogi and Other Medieval Welsh Tales*.

Berkeley: University of California Press.

———, ed. 1992. *Ystoria Taliesin.* Cardiff: University of Wales Press.

Gantz, Timothy. 1993. *Early Greek Myth: A Guide to Literary and Artistic Sources. Volume One.* Baltimore and London: The Johns Hopkins University Press.

Gerow, Bert. 1950. "Bloodclot Boy: An Historical and Stylistic Study of a North American Indian Hero Tale." PhD thesis, University of California, Berkeley.

Gulermovich Epstein, Angelique. 1994. "Miscarriages and Miraculous Births in Indo-European Tradition." *Journal of Indo-European Studies* 22 (1-2): 151–63.

van Hamel, A. G., ed. 1978. *Compert Con Culainn.* Dublin: Dublin Institute for Advanced Studies.

Hemming, Jessica. 1998. "Reflections on Rhiannon and the Horse Episodes in 'Pwyll'." *Western Folklore* 57 (1): 19–40.

Jamison, Stephanie W. 1991. *The Ravenous Hyenas and the Wounded Sun: Myth and Ritual in Ancient India.* Ithaca: Cornell University Press.

Jamison, Stephanie W. and Joel P. Brereton, trans. 2014. *The Rigveda. The Earliest Religious Poetry of India.* 3 volumes. Oxford: Oxford University Press.

Johnston, Sarah Iles. 2013. "The Myth of Dionysus." In *Ritual Texts for the Afterlife: Orpheus and the Bacchic Gold Tablets*, 2nd ed., edited by Fritz Graf and Sarah Iles Johnston, 66–93. New York: Routledge.

Jones, Leslie Ellen. 2005. "Boys in Boxes: The Recipe for a Welsh Hero." In *Heroic Poets and Poetic Heroes in Celtic Tradition: A Festschrift for Patrick K. Ford*, edited by Joseph Falaky Nagy and Leslie Ellen Jones, 207–25. Dublin: Four Courts.

Liddell, Henry George and Robert Scott. 1940. *A Greek-English Lexicon.* Oxford: Clarendon.

Mac Cana, Proinsias. 1970. *Celtic Mythology.* London: Hamlyn.

McCone, Kim. 1990. *Pagan Past and Christian Present in Early Irish Literature.* Maynooth: Department of Old Irish, National University of Ireland, Maynooth.

Ó Cathasaigh, Tomás. 1985. "The Concept of the Hero in Irish Mythology." In *The Irish Mind: Exploring Intellectual Traditions*, edited by R. Kearney, 79–90. Dublin: Wolfhound Press.

Oldfather, C. H., ed. and trans. (1935) 2006. *Diodorus of Sicely: The Library of History. Books II.35-IV.58.* Cambridge, MA: Harvard University Press.

Pagé, Anna June. 2014. "Birth Narratives in Indo-European Mythology." PhD thesis, University of California, Los Angeles.

Roberts, Brynley F., ed. 1975. *Cyfranc Lludd a Llefelys.* Dublin: Dublin Institute for Advanced Studies.

Roider, Ulrike, ed. and trans. 1979. *De Chophur in Dá Muccida.* Innsbruck: Innsbrucker Beiträge zur Sprachwissenschaft.

Rose, H. I., ed. 1933. *Hygini Fabulae.* Leiden: A. W. Sythoff.

Thompson, Stith. 1929. *Tales of the North American Indians.* Cambridge, MA: Harvard University Press.

Thurneysen, Rudolf. 1921. *Die irische Helden- und Königsage bis zum siebzehnten Jahrhundert. Teil I und II.* Halle (Saale): Max Niemeyer.

Wagner, Richard, ed. 1965. *Mythographi Graeci Vol. I: Apollodori Bibliotheca.* Stuttgart: B. G. Teubner.

West, M. L. 1983. *The Orphic Poems.* Oxford: Clarendon.

―――. 2007. *Indo-European Poetry and Myth.* Oxford: Oxford University Press.

Williams, Ifor, ed. 1964. *Pedeir Keinc Y Mabinogi.* Caerdydd: Gwasg Prifyscol Cymru.

Sticky Figures: The Afterlife of Pre-Christian Supernatural Beings in Medieval Celtic Texts

DANIEL F. MELIA

ABSTRACT.*Surviving Medieval Welsh and Irish vernacular narratives, although generally set in a pseudo-historical legendary past, often involve clearly mythological figures from what must be a much older tradition. Some characters keep well-known divine names, like Lug, or Mabon ap Modron while others keep only obvious functional or iconographic features (Rhiannon < Epona). I argue that there are three major categories, or ways of asserting value, that largely explain this phenomenon: orderliness (depiction of an orderly and explainable ancient past congruent with the polity of the present of the story tellers); origins (the display of the antiquity of the ideal present polity, establishing direct connection between the present dynasts and their remotest ancestors); and ostentation (holding forth of claims to special privilege in the present by connection to or analogy with the deep past).*

KEYWORDS: *Wales, Ireland, Mythology, Legend, Mabinogi, Pwyll, Rhiannon, Dyfed.*

Sometimes the gods stick around as mere expressions (*By Jove!*) sometimes frozen into place names (*Lyon* or *Leiden* < *Lugudunum,* "fortified place/height of the god Lug"), sometimes as detached metaphors (Pandora's Box). What I concerns me here, though, is the appearance of pre-Christian gods in medieval Celtic narratives, either as recognizable names (Lug mac Ethlenn, Nuadu, Mabon ap Modron, Manawyden), or as recognizable mythological figures such as Rhiannon, or The Dagda. In particular, what might be called "time-sliding" occurs in at least two branches of the *Mabinogi* (text, Williams, 1989; trans. Ford, 1977), wherein figures from the imagined pre-Christian world mingle either with Christians, or with historically Christian settings. In *Manawydan*, the tale's eponym interacts with a priest and a bishop in the episode of the enchanted rapacious mice, and in *Branwyn*, Bran instructs his followers to (eventually) bury his head, facing France (*Freinc,* the traditional enemy?) at the Tower of London, implying not only a Christian time-frame, but a time not unadjacent to the Hundred Years' War (i.e. post-1337, about coeval with the White Book, the earlier of the two manuscripts of the *Mabinogi*; MS: National Library of Wales; Huws, 2000).

In our own era, after *Tristram Shandy*, Surrealism, Dada, magical

Figure 1. Illustration of Hill of Narberth. Photo: visitwales.com

in the eyes of a *Guardian* book reviewer, but, given the shape of what survives to us of medieval narrative in Celtic languages, the intermixing of Christian and pre-Christian worlds in the *Mabinogi* narratives is striking and deserves some comment. Let me start by examining the complex of motifs and references surrounding the character of Rhiannon in the *Mabinogi*. Why, after a thousand years of Christianity, does such a character persist in Welsh legendary narrative?

In the first branch of the *Mabinogi* our initial protagonist, Pwyll, having earned the title *Pen Annwfn* ("Chief of the Otherworld") by exchanging his kingdom with the supernatural being Arawn, seeks a wife, the natural next stage in this story of maturation into sovereignty:

> One time he was in Arberth, his chief court, and a feast had been prepared for him and the great numbers of men with him. After the first sitting Pwyll rose to take a walk, and proceeded to the top of a mound that was just above the court, called the Mound of Arberth.

> "Lord," said a member of the court, "it is a characteristic of the mound that any noble who sits upon it shall not leave it without the one of two things: either he will be wounded, or suffer an injury, or he will see a marvel." (Ford 1977, 42)

What Pwyll sees from the mound (cf. Fig. 1) is a richly dressed woman riding a "majestic" (*aruchel*) pale-white horse slowly along the main road by the Mound. Pwyll sends servants out to accost the woman, the second of whom "put spurs to his horse, but the more he spurred the horse, the farther she would be from him." The chase is repeated the next day with

Figure 2. Epona from Champoulet (Loiret, Centre, France). Photo: Joffroy 1978.

identical results. On the third day, Pwyll himself takes up the futile chase until, in exasperation, he calls out to her: "Maiden, for the sake of the man you love most, wait for me." "I will gladly," she said, "and it had been better for the horse if you had asked it long ago." She then acknowledges that she has come specifically to see Pwyll and identifies herself as "Rhiannon, daughter of Hyfaidd Hên," and asserts that she is being married against her will to another man, but that she loves only Pwyll (Ford 1977, 44-45).

This introduction of Rhiannon puts the audience immediately in the legendary past world of early British, and, as I assert later, common Celtic culture. First, in a story in which the question of fitness for sovereignty has already been raised, Rhiannon fits into the established thematic narrative slot of the sovereignty goddess of the locality who must be symbolically wed to the head of the tribe. The Uí Néill dynastic origin story, *The Adventures of the Sons of Eochaid Mugmedhon* (Stokes 1903), explains how the youngest son, because of his willingness to sleep with the "loathly lady," gains the sovereignty that she has to offer. Likewise, the royal inauguration story related by Gerald of Wales in his *Itinerary of Ireland*, involving the king-to-be mating with a mare and then consuming her flesh, points to Rhiannon as a nexus of a variety of beliefs about pre-Christian deities (Gerald of Wales 1982). Owing to her magical horse, Rhiannon has often been equated with the well-known Gaulish deity Epona ("Ms. Equine Animal"; cf. Fig. 2).

Rhiannon's equine connections are emphasized in her later unjust punishment for allegedly killing her infant son carrying visitors on her back to the court, and by her means of confinement, wearing a horse collar, during her magical disappearance into the otherworld in *Manawydan*.

Additionally, her son Gwri (later renamed Pryderi) has a horse which he begins to care for when he is a small boy. Her appropriateness as a sovereignty goddess is apparent both in her name, Rhiannon < *rigantona "great queen" or "possessor of queenliness" (cf. the Irish battle goddess Morrigan, perhaps < mor + rigain, "great queen"), and in her demand to marry Pwyll, rather than the husband her father, Hyfaidd Hên, had chosen for her, Gwawl ap Clud.

Rhiannon's status as a goddess of horses as well as of sovereignty seems metaphorically historically appropriate for a semi-nomadic tribal people, who defined their polity by lineage rather than by geography. It is notable that, until the end of the Middle Irish period, most Irish tribal names were declinable names of peoples, rather than of territories. For example, the first line of the originally ninth century Scél mucce meicc dathó (The Story of MacDatho's Pig), is Boí rí amra for Laignib, .i. Mac Dathó a ainm ("There was a famous king over the Leinstermen [dative pl.] namely, Mac Datho"; Thurneysen 1935). In such a social context, the mythic mating of the incoming royal lineage and the stationary goddess of the place is a perfect metaphor.

These mythic and legendary motifs seem particularly appropriate in the setting of Pwyll, which is a sort of royal Bildungsroman, in which Pwyll, who starts with the title of Pendefig Dyfed, "Chieftain/Prince of Dyfed," actually earns the title while learning the necessary steps to become a proper sovereign. He learns from his mistakes: first, insulting a king of the otherworld, Arawn, and atoning by successfully fulfilling the role of king of the otherworld in Arawn's place; second, by learning to approach the sovereignty goddess politely, rather than just chasing her down; third, by listening to the advice of Rhiannon, his fiancé, after he has interrupted what were to be his own nuptials by offering a particularly dimwitted rash boon (are there smart rash boons?) to Rhiannon's previous betrothed, Gwawl; fourth, by ultimately acknowledging his too-easy acceptance of Rhiannon's apparent guilt in the disappearance (alleged murder) of their son, and then by appointing proper foster parents for the boy after his rediscovery.

Myth and legend do not survive unless they continue somehow to serve some audience, and, on the level of what we might call "authorizing metaphor", the tale of Pwyll and Rhiannon can be seen to have relevance in twelfth- and thirteenth-century Wales. The Edwardian Reconquista of the thirteenth century had left the native Welsh nobility scattered and demoralized; narratives emphasizing native conceptions of sovereignty and legitimacy would have had a certain appeal to a Welsh speaking audience (Morris 2008).

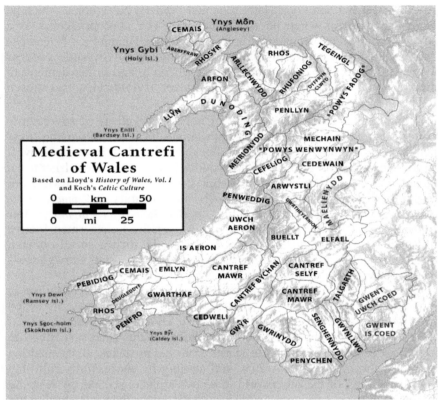

Figure 3. Cantrefs of Medieval Wales. Photo: wikipedia.org.

Thus, metaphoric aptness is an element of "stickiness" in this case and cases like it. Historically illustrative and/or metaphoric stories and story patterns connected to pre-Christian deities and otherworld figures find continuing use, because they provide orderliness to the imagining of the relationship of the past to the present. The ultimate appeal in Roman argumentation, after all, was to the *mos maiorum*, "the custom of our ancestors."

There is also a geographic aspect to the tale of Pwyll and Rhiannon. To begin with, Pwyll is "Lord over the seven cantrefs of Dyfed" (*Pwyll, Pendefig Dyfed a oed yn arglwyd ar seith cantref Dyfed*; Williams 1; Ford 1977, 37). These were, namely, Emlyn, Cemais, Gwarthaf, Penfro, Deugleddyf, Pebidiog, and Rhos (Fig. 3).

By the end of the First Branch, Dyfed also encompasses the three Cantrefs of Tywi: Cantref Mawr, Cantref Bychan, and Cedweli. Plus, by alliance, Teyrnyon in Gwent is Coed. And also, the four Cantrefs of Ceredigion: Is Aeron, Uch Aeron, Buellt, and Penweddig.

Rhiannon identifies herself as the daughter of Hyffaid Hên, "Hyffaid the Old," or, better, the lineage-founding ancestor, as Patrick Ford has argued (1970). Compare the use of Mór in Irish. There was a historical Hyffaid, son of Bleddri, who ruled Dyfed in the ninth century. According to Triad 68, he was one of the three kings sprung from peasant stock (*veibion eillion*). Rachel Bromwich has argued that, as in the case of the famous Merfyn Vrych (825-44), the first Welsh King of Gwynedd not claiming descent from Cunedda, Hyfaidd claimed kingship through his mother, which seems metaphorically orthogonal here (Bromwich 2006). I would not argue that Rhiannon's father is necessarily meant to be that Hyfaidd, but the association of the name with the kingdom of Dyfed is, I think, the point here. The name of her father links her to the land of Dyfed, underlining her role as a local sovereignty goddess.

Her otherworldly suitor, Gwawl ap Clud, "Wall (?) son of the River Clyde" is presumably from farther north. He might represent a long-lasting literary trace of the British Kingdom of Strathclyde, or an atavistic name amongst the Gwyr y Gogledd, the "Men of the North" (Cunedda and his descendants) who dominated the rule of Gwynedd, and thus much of Wales, after migrating from Strathclyde and Rheged during the Middle Ages (Davies 1989; Bromwich 2006). My own guess is that the name is a learned joke ("Hadrian's Wall, son of the River Clyde").

The closing lines of *Pwyll* underscore the geographical interest of the text: "In this way years and years passed until Pwyll Pen Annwfn's life ended and he died. And then Pryderi [his son] ruled the seven cantrefs of Dyfed successfully . . . later he gained the three cantrefs of Ystrad Tywi [Cantref Mawr, Cantref Bychan, Cedweli] and the four cantrefs of Ceredigion [Is Aeron, Uch Aeron, Buellt, Penweddig]; these are called the seven cantrefs of Seisyllwch" (Ford 56). And we can add to this list Gwent Is Coed, the territory of Pryderi's foster father Teyrnyon. A look at the map (Fig. 3) illustrates the territorial claims in South Wales that are attached to Rhiannon, Pwyll and Pryderi. If, as has been conjectured, one of the motives for Iolo Morgannwg's eighteenth-century forgeries of medieval Welsh materials was his desire to provide a legendary and literary history for Glamorganshire (medieval Glywysing), perhaps in *Pwyll* we see a similar attempt to shore up the credentials of South Wales by providing useful origin stories. I would argue that Rhiannon's connection to the geography of South Wales is another part of her stickiness. The alleged accumulation of historical territories would fall under a second element of stickiness to go with *orderliness*: origins.

Figure 4. Stone of Divisions, Hill of Uisnech. Photo: Ali Isaac.

Where does authority come from? It comes from ancestry, from knowing the deeds of your own forebears as well as your own. Aristotle said that the *polis* was not the physical fabric of the city-state, or its geographical boundaries, but rather the citizens' shared story of the history and the purposes of the *polis* (*Politics*, 3). Virgil provided the Julian rulers of Rome with an origin story in the *Aeneid*, and, closer to home, Geoffrey of Monmouth provided a similar origin story for the sovereignty of Britain—the Britain ruled by the newly implanted Plantagenets (Wright 1984).

We see a similar attention to *origins* and *orderliness* in medieval Irish material. The Ulster Cycle tales are set in the pseudo-historical Pentarchy of the pseudo-historical year one. The very setting of the notion of five provinces with a central point is, itself, almost certainly pan-Celtic and possibly pan-Indo-European (Rees and Rees 1978). Caesar says that the Gaulish druids met each year in the territory of the Carnutes (today, I would bet my house, on the site of the Cathedral of Chartres) which, Caesar says, "they consider to be the centre of Gaul" (*De bello Gallico* VI). The Hill of Uisnech fills a similar purpose in Ireland with its "Stone of Divisions" (Fig. 4).

The place name Milan (from **medio-lanum*, "middle place") may be a remnant of a similar place designation. Of course, the *omphalos* at Delphi seems to be the same idea. Rees and Rees make a case that the arrangement of the world into five zones: four peripheral and one central, is a fundamental Indo-European schema. As such, its continuation into later legend is both an element of stickiness and an example of why it is sticky: *it organizes the matrix of the world and can be put to use as an origin legend.* The introduction of Christianity and writing, and, as a result, the entire ancient and biblical history of the world, had to be integrated into their own fully developed history of the world by the Irish and Welsh. The traditional world of the native gods provided a stable base, a local origin story, and an authenticating set of narratives that distinguished their own local history from that of the rest of the Christian world.

Characters such as Lugh mac Ethlenn and Fergus mac Roech are pretty straightforwardly gods. Cú Chulainn, Conchobor, Ailill, Conall Cernach, and the other "heroes" like Pwyll and Pryderi, seem to be seriously intermixed with the gods of the otherworld, either by maternity or paternity (Cú Chulainn, Pryderi), by exploits or attributes (Pwyll, who substitutes for the King of the Otherworld, or Fergus who is both Cú Chulainn's foster father, and an exemplar of druidic knowledge and practice when he decodes *ogam* and the like), or by special names (Conchobor mac Nessa, Ailill mac Mata, and Lugh mac Ethlenn, at a minimum, have matronymics).

My late Berkeley colleague Professor William Bascomb famously proposed a structural distinction between "myth" and "legend": "myths" are narratives that take place in the time before the creation of the ordinary world of history, while "legends" are narratives set in the present world, even if they involve supernatural beings or elements (1965). Thus, by his definition, the *Book of Genesis* is myth, while the rest of the Old and New Testament is legend; Hesiod's *Theogony* is myth, while the Homeric epics are legend.[1]

There are, of course, many other ways to look at the terms "myth" and "mythology." An important definition is a functional one: a myth is a narrative upon which some people feel (or once felt) compelled to model or modify their behaviour. By this definition, the entire *Bible* constitutes myth, as do, say, the *Bhagavad Gita*, and the *Koran*. I use or allude to both these definitions.

When we speak of myth and legend, even when the narratives in question have many living believers, we are almost always speaking of *reception phenomena*, since most narratives achieve mythic or legendary status only with the passage of time. Even in the case of recently developed mythologies, we seldom have direct access to their creators. The Bahá'u'lláh, Joseph Smith, and even L. Ron Hubbard are unavailable for interview. In the case of the medieval Celtic world, as with the medieval Germanic world and no doubt many others, we have a case of (at least) double reception: first, a fully comprehensive set of pre-Christian origin stories (now, alas, surviving mainly in fragments and references) and second, the competing set of mythical, legendary, pseudo-historical and historical beliefs ushered in by Christianity.

An excellent example of this process (and the interpenetration of Irish and British learned lore) occurs at the end of the Second Branch of the *Mabinogi, Branwen, Daughter of Llyr.* After Bran and his followers have defeated the Irish, avenged the treatment of Branwen by Matholwch, and returned to Wales, the text reports,

> In Ireland none were left alive except five pregnant women in a cave in the wastes of Ireland. And these five women simultaneously bore five sons. They raised these five boys until they were big lads, who turned their thoughts on women, and desired to have them. And then they slept, in turn, with each other's mother, and they inhabited the land and dwelt in it, dividing it among the five of them. They still call the five districts from that division (Ford 72).

This passage is taken directly from the massive (and unfinished) medieval Irish pseudo-historical work called the *Lebor Gabala,* the *Book of Invasions,* begun in the tenth century (Macalister 1938). The passage is part of an attempt to reconcile native Irish lore with the Biblical story of the Flood. What we find in *Branwen* is an appropriation of the story, not to explain how Ireland was repopulated after Noah's Flood, but that the war between Bran and Matholwch was the origin of the legendary Pentarchy of the Ulster sagas. As such, like the Ulster cycle narratives, the stories and characters in the *Mabinogi* collection take place just at the interface between mythic and legendary time, in Bascomb's terms. Characters like Bran, Rhiannon, Manawydan and the other Children of Llyr, Mabon, Cú Chulainn, Fergus mac Roech, Conchobor mac Nessa, and Ailill mac Mata are, one might say, either last generation gods or first generation humans. It may be notable in this regard that characters from this pseudo-historical stratum, such as Conchobor and Ailill have, as I have mentioned, matronymics rather than patronymics. This particular intersection brings up a third feature of stickiness with respect to pre-Christian worldview: *ostentation*, the holding forth of claims to special privilege in the present by connection to or analogy with the deep past.

If I am right about the first three branches of the *Mabinogi* as concerned with asserting pseudo-historical claims about the sovereignty of Seisyllwg, we can see the same phenomenon in the reception of the Ulster Cycle. The original Ulaid, probably the *Oulouti* of Ptolemy's second century map of Ireland (Darcy and Flynn 2008), were the tribe called the Dál Fiatach, but, by the seventh century, the ethnonym had been claimed by the resurgent Dál nAraidi. Donnchadh O'Corrain's recent paper (2015) argued cogently that some of the Irish genealogies contain material dating back to the time of Ptolemy's map, which would mean that they were preserving material that had been in oral form for 300 years at a minimum, before Christianity brought writing to Ireland.

I have called the medieval Irish intellectuals' attempt to reconcile the new facts brought in with Christianity with their own highly developed and presumably coherent native lore "The Big Project," and it clearly occupied the efforts of countless medieval Irishmen (and perhaps some Irishwomen) from around 550 CE through the fifteenth century. Similar efforts may have been undertaken in Britain but we have even less direct evidence from the Big Island than we do from Ireland.

The process of assimilating the old mythology to the new is exemplified by the material in the Irish law tracts, which, when written down in the seventh century, consciously incorporated much material from the Old Testament as evidence of the righteousness of their ancestors (Binchy 1978). For example, the tracts on marriage justify parallel cousin marriage between rich women and poorer men of their same kindred by explicit reference to the story of the daughters of Salphaad in Leviticus (O'Corrain 1998). The early ninth-century retrospective pseudo-preface to the major seventh-century Irish law tract, the *Senchas Már* ("The Great Lore"), provides both an example of this process of reception/incorporation and an explanation of the process itself in the law tracts:

> For the Holy Spirit spoke and prophesied through the mouths of the righteous men who were first in the island of Ireland, as He prophesied through the mouths of the chief prophets and patriarchs in the law of the Old Testament; for the law of nature reached many things which the law of scripture did not reach. As for the judgments of true nature which the Holy Spirit uttered through the mouths of the righteous judges and poets of the men of Ireland,

from the time when this island was settled until the coming of the faith: Dubhtach revealed them all to Patrick. Whatever did not go against God's word in the law of scripture and in the New Testament, or against the consciences of the faithful, was fixed in the system of judgment by Patrick and the churches and the princes of Ireland severally. The law of nature was acceptable, save (in what concerns) the faith, and its proper dues, and the knitting together of church and kingdom. So that that is the *Senchas Már.* (Carey 143)

While anachronistic, this passage probably correctly iterates the actual process of accommodating native material to Christian and other European and Mediterranean history and culture.

Unlike the exceptionally meagre medieval Welsh prose tradition, Irish has a "mythological cycle" dealing with acknowledged pre-Christian gods such as Nuadu, Lug and Balor, not to mention The Dagda. Our primary surviving document is *The Second Battle of Moytura*, a kind of War of the Aesir and Vanir, in which the Fomorian, Bres, having become king over the Tuatha Dé Dannan, has a disastrous reign characterized by drought and famine (Gray 1982). Nuada of the silver arm, the former king, is killed in a battle with the one-eyed giant Balor during a revolt against Bres, but Lugh defeats Balor and Bres is taken prisoner. But here is the interesting part: the terms for ransoming Bres are that he reveal the secrets of agriculture (when to sow, when to reap etc.) Why should a king who has presided over drought and famine be expected to give up the secrets of agriculture? The Dumézilian answer is that Bres was trying to fulfill the wrong function as King. If he is an expert in agriculture, he is properly a third function figure and his serving as a first function figure as king would cause retribution from the land and thus famine (Littleton 1973).

That these openly mythological tales should continue to exist in medieval Ireland is interesting in itself, but more interesting is that they form a background to the pseudo-historical stage of the Ulster Cycle, in which the motif of the substitute king who becomes permanent (Conchobor for Fergus = Bres for the damaged Nuada), and the hero Cú Chulainn (birth name Sétanta: "the one who knows routes") share the supernatural attributes of his "real" father Lugh (a god of routes and roads equivalent to Mercury, according to Caesar; *De bello Galico* VI). The recapitulation of actual mythological narrative is a characteristic of medieval Irish as well as of Welsh.

Figure 5. Undercroft of Church of St. Melar, Lanmeur Melar, Brittany. Photo: infobretagne. com

Nuadu, himself, has had an interesting mythological afterlife. As a god, he lost his arm (like the Norse Tyr, and, if Dumézil is correct in identifying Gaius Mucius Scaevola with the Roman Dius Fidius, with Dius Fidius as well) but had it replaced by a better one in silver. He is equivalent to the Romano-British Nodens, whose temple of healing at Lydney Park in Gloucester was excavated by a team including J.R.R. Tolkien (Wheeler and Wheeler 1932). And he ends up as a Breton saint, St. Melar, whose wicked uncle wounded and deposed him from his kingship, but who had his arm miraculously replaced. This is sticky indeed. His chief cult is in the parish of Lanmeur in Finistère (cf. Fig. 5). He was also venerated in England (as St. Melor).

Three fundamental literary critical questions that need to be asked of any text are: 1) what is going on? 2) why does it matter? (to its original audience) and 3) why should *we* care? What is going on in these medieval Celtic tales is both simple and complicated. The story lines are relatively simple (if bizarre in the case of the four branches of the *Mabinogi*) but individual incidents are from a variety of genres and sources: Indo-European epic patterns in the *Tain Bo Cuailnge* (like the *Iliad* from the Trojan point of view); international folktale in the case of the plague of enchanted mice; native onomastics in the case of Welsh *Tal Ebolion* ("End of the Ridges" not, as the tale *Branwen* has it, "the counting of the horses"), or the Irish *Slechta*, ("the hewn place," but with two competing onomastic origins given in the *Cattle Raid of Cooley*; O'Rahilly 123); the Welsh and Irish triads (Manawydan as one of the three noble shoemakers in Triad 67, the striking of Branwen as one of the three most grievous blows, Triad 53; Bromwich); and genealogy, or at least pseudo-genealogy (Hefaidd Hên, Conchobor mac Nessa, son of Cathbad).

One of the other things that is going on in the *Mabinogi* is the attempt to establish a coherent picture of the earliest stages of civil polity in south-western Wales. It must be of the earliest stages because it involves interactions between humans and pre-Christian deities. Earlier, and you are in the realm of pure mythology (such as the aforementioned *Second Battle of Moytura*); later, you are in the realm of the ordinary. These tales are set in an important liminal period, and, I would argue, that is one of the reasons that the tales were important to their own original audience. While not directly ancestral to later medieval people, the existence of this period anchors later genealogical material on the secular side. I learned only recently that Llywelen ap Gruffud actually wrote a letter to Henry III claiming that Wales was independent because he, Llywelen, was directly descended from Kamber, the son of Geoffrey of Monmouth's Brutus of Troy, whose portion was Wales (Locrinum was over England and Albanias over Scotland). So, in the thirteenth century, the political usefulness of a pseudo-historical genealogy is clear (Edwards 1935).

The original cultures did care about these materials and seemingly had good reason to do so. They provided origins, orderliness, and ostentation. These are largely narratives of a particular pseudo-historical time, when the gods intermingled with ordinary men, and, as such, could offer a kind of grounded, shared world-view regarding pre-Christian or non-Christian, or Christian times in vernacular history. As to why *we* should care, I offer the notion that we, too, have been partially made who we are culturally by these same fictions.

Like the ancient Celts at La Tène, we still throw precious metal into water (Fig. 6) and only places with a Celtic substrate and/or Celtic immigration do this. Africans and Chinese do not.

There are, of course, some other recognizable forms of stickiness: Nuadu *Argetlamh* (= Nodens) is eventually transmogrified into St. Melar who holds his unrestored hand in its replacement, echoing his mythological ancestor and his association with healing chthonic powers. The TRINOX SAMON SINDIU of the first century Calendar of Coligny (Fig. 7) survives as Samhain/Halloween.

Figure 6. Pool in Luxor hotel, Las Vegas, NV. Photo: Daniel F. Melia.

Figure 7: Calendar of Coligny (detail). Photo: lila.sns.it

In his *Wahrheit und Methode* (1960) Hans-Georg Gadamer stresses the importance of tradition. He claims (following Heidegger) that a fundamental unity exists between thought, language and the world. It is through language that the horizon of the "now" comes into being. This language, however, is always marked by the past. Through language the past lives on in the present and thus represents tradition. According to Gadamer, the Enlightenment made an important mistake when it failed to take these "prejudices" and traditions seriously: the burden of the past was too easily discarded. Gadamer claims that it is tradition which shapes our ways of understanding and interpreting the world through language. And this tradition, he is well aware, does not exist of itself. It must constantly be embraced, confirmed and cultivated. It also requires (but Gadamer doesn't tell us this) reinterpretation and pure make-belief. (Holthof 1996).

I have elsewhere characterized this kind of traditional "stickiness" as "cultural intention," which often overrides the personal intentions of the carrier of the narrative (Melia 1979).

Not all traditions seem to have the particular kind of stickiness we see in Irish and Welsh medieval material. Outside of Eddic poetry and Snorri Sturluson's highly synthetic fourteenth *Heimskringla,* Old Norse does not seem to have the same kind of survival of the gods. Hesiod, and Homer represent a similar kind of tradition, which survives in the Classical world for many of the same reasons, I think: providing a set of foundational narratives that continue to make sense of the fundamental structure of the cultures over time. The continuation of classical mythology by authors such as Ovid and Virgil gives evidence of the cultural validity of these ancient stories.

There is a reason, though, why we find the particular kind of stickiness in medieval Celtic narrative. I blame it on the druids. Perhaps because Christianity came late to Ireland and parts of Britain, its learned class, which, like the Brahmin caste in India was responsible for history, religion, astronomy, and the other learned arts, remained fully functioning and in control of their native material until the early Middle Ages, and even continued in traditional pre-Christian professions within official Christianity. With the coming of Christianity, this class did not go away, as is evidenced by the genealogies, law tracts, king lists, *dindshenchus, banshenchus* triads and narratives. Much of the material produced orally enters the written traditions of these cultures and preserves both earlier details, and a general picture of the world. So long as that picture seems useful in the present (whatever present that is), it is retold.

Daniel F. Melia is Associate Professor Emeritus of Rhetoric and Celtic Studies at University of California Berkeley.

Notes

1   Leaving aside the casual use of the word myth to mean "something stupid you believe that I do not" (calling to mind Bishop Warburton's quip to the fourth Earl of Sandwich: "orthodoxy is my doxy, heterodoxy is another man's doxy"; Priestley I, 572).

References

Bascomb, William. 1965. "The Forms of Folklore: Prose Narratives." *The Journal of American Folklore* 78 (307): 3-20.

Binchy, Daniel, ed. 1978. *Corpus iuris Hibernici: ad fidem codicum manuscriptorum.* Dublin: Institute for Advanced Studies.

Bromwich, Rachel, ed. and tr. 2006. *Trioedd Ynys Prydein.* Cardiff: University of Wales Press. (plus: Appendix II *Bonhed Gwyr y Gogled* pp. 256-7 < pen. 45.)

Carey, John. 1998. "The Pseudo-Historical Prologue to the Senchas Már." In *King of Mysteries, Early Irish Religious Writings,* edited by John Carey, 140-144. Dublin: Four Courts Press.

Darcy, R. and William Flynn. 2008. "Ptolemy's map of Ireland: a modern decoding." *Irish Geography* 41 (1): 49-69.

Davies, Wendy. 1989. *Wales in the Early Middle Ages.* Leicester: Leicester University Press.

Edwards, J. Goronwy, ed. 1935. *Calendar of Ancient Correspondence Concerning Wales.* Cardiff: University of Wales Press.

Ford, Patrick. trans. 1977. *The Mabinogi and Other Medieval Welsh Tales.* Berkeley: University of California Press.

Ford, Patrick. 1970. "Llywarch, Ancestor of Welsh Princes." *Speculum* 45 (3): 442–50.

Gadamer, Hans-Georg. 1960. *Wahrheit und Methode*. Tübingen: J.C.B. Mohr.

Gerald of Wales. [ca. 1188] 1982. *The History and Topography of Ireland*. Translated by John J. O'Meara. Harmondsworth: Penguin.

Gray, Elizabeth, ed. and trans. 1982. *Cath Maige Tuired: The Second Battle of Mag Tuired* . Dublin: Irish Texts Society.

Hanoteau, Marie-Thérèse. 1979. "Sur les traces d'Epona dans le Centre de la France." *Revue archéologique du Centre de la France* 18 (3): 157-159.

Holthof, Marc. 1996, May 21. "The Prince Consort's New Clothes". *Nettime* (online mailing list) http://www.nettime.org/Lists-Archives/nettime-l-9605/msg00042.html

Huws, D. 2000. "Llyfr Gwyn Rhydderch." In *Medieval Welsh Manuscripts*, 227-68. Cardiff & Aberystwyth: University of Wales Press.

Joffroy, René. 1978. *Découverte d'une cachette de bronzes gallo-romains à Champoulet (Loiret)*. Paris: Comptes rendus de l'académie des inscriptions et belles-lettres.

Littleton, C. Scott. 1973. *The New Comparative Mythology: An Anthropological Assessment of the Theories of Georges Dumézil*. Berkeley CA: University of California Press.

Macalister, R.A.S. 1938 et seq. *Lebor gabála Érenn: The book of the taking of Ireland*. Dublin: Irish Texts Society.

Melia, Daniel F. 1979. "Some Remarks on the Affinities of Medieval Irish Saga," *Acta Antiqua Academiae Scientiarum Hungaricae* 27: 255-261.

Morris, Marc. 2008. *A Great and Terrible King: Edward I and the Forging of Britain*. London: Hutchinson.

Ó Corráin, Donnchadh. 1998. "Creating the Past: The Early Irish Genealogical Tradition (Carroll Lecture 1992)." *Peritia* 12:177–208

O'Corrain, Donnchadh. 2015 "Genealogies and Origin Legends: Contradictions and Subversions." Paper presented at the XV International Congress of Celtic Studies, University of Glasgow, 12-17 July.

O'Rahilly, Cecile, ed. and tr. 1976. *Táin Bó Cúailnge Recension I*. Dublin: Institute for Advanced Studies.

Priestley, Joseph. 1809. *Memoires*. Vol. I, 572. London: Allenson.

Rees, Alwyn D., and B. R. Rees. 1978. *Celtic heritage: ancient tradition in Ireland and Wales*. London: Thames and Hudson.

Stokes, Whitley, ed. and tr. 1903. "The death of Crimthann son of Fidach, and

38

Daniel F. Melia

the adventures of the sons of Eochaid Muigmedón." *Revue Celtique* 24: 172–207, 446 (add. and corr.)

Thurneysen, Rudolf, ed. 1935. *Scéla mucce Meic Dathó*, Mediaeval and Modern Irish Series 6, Dublin: Dublin Institute for Advanced Studies.

Williams, Ifor. ed. 1989. *Pedeir Keinc y Mabinogi*. Cardiff: University of Wales Press.

Wheeler, R.E. M. and T.V. Wheeler. 1932. "Report on the Excavation of the Prehistoric, Roman, and Post-Roman Site in Lydney Park, Gloucestershire." *Reports of the Research Committee of the Society of Antiquaries of London.* IX. Oxford: Oxford University Press for the Society of Antiquaries.

White Book of Rhydderch. National Library of Wales, MS Peniarth 4. https://www.llgc.org.uk/?id=256.

Wright, N. ed. 1984. *The Historia regum Britannie of Geoffrey of Monmouth.* 1, Bern, Burgerbibliothek, MS. 568. Cambridge: D.S. Brewer.

Scottish Traditional Tales: Distributions and Prehistory*

JOHN SHAW

ABSTRACT. *The use of increasingly sophisticated technologies and wider fields of comparison have enabled researchers to explore the history of tales in a considerably deeper timeframe than was heretofore possible. The linking of such extended comparisons with genetic evidence has begun to lead to a clearer understanding of the migration of tales. Central to this progress has been the work of Yuri Berezkin and his studies interpreting the global distribution of 'motifs'. His results, available online in distribution maps and interpreted in his publications, provide the potential for a new perspective on long-standing questions regarding the history of Scottish storytelling traditions: How old are our stories and what are their origins? This essay briefly surveys the history of research into the origins of folktales, and views Scotland's part in this through the work of the Victorian folktale collector John Francis Campbell and advances over the past few decades. Following this is a selection from a list of items from our archived collections and fieldwork, together with their geographical distributions and comments, compiled earlier by the writer, with a view to supplementing Berezkin's data for Scotland.*

KEYWORDS: *folktales, Scotland, prehistory, comparative mythology.*

THE STUDY OF SCOTTISH FOLKTALES AND PREHISTORY

Methodical research into the history and prehistory of folktales began with the Brothers Grimms' publication in 1812 of their pioneering and influential collection *Kinder- und Hausmärchen*. In their 1856 edition of the work, they outline the similarities between tales of different peoples, the connections and affinities that can be inferred from these, and what they reveal of the history and prehistory of tales. The Grimms' declared approach (for English translation, see Thompson 1949, 368-71) followed on the discoveries in the field of comparative philology successfully developed

* My grateful thanks to Yuri Berezkin for generously providing the images for the motifs discussed.

from the late eighteenth century, by use of the 'comparative method' central to historical linguistics and comparative mythology. In the area of Indo-European, where language-based comparisons have been most intensively studied, their application to folktales, putatively extending our view back as far as Common Indo-European times, even gave rise to the attempt by August Schleicher in 1868 to reconstruct a folktale in Indo-European.

However such a direct and enthusiastic attempt is viewed in our day, within 40 years the groundwork for comparison of folktales was beginning to be laid. From 1907, the Folklore Fellows monographs provided useful and reliable histories based on oral, printed and manuscript sources of some of the better-known international folktales. In these wide-ranging studies, sometimes covering vast geographical distances, the search for origins remained paramount. It was complemented by abundant evidence demonstrating the ability of tales to travel and change under a wide variety of circumstances, and the extent to which cultures and language groups are connected under the surface, as it were, by widespread shared traditions. Some recent works have likewise successfully pushed back the timeframe for folktale scholarship by providing access to and interpretation of the earliest written sources for folktales. Drawing on the most ancient written sources from Egypt, Palestine and Mesopotamia, Heda Jason (1981) has shown how they contain tales well-known in traditions recorded millennia later in Europe; William Hansen (2002) has related the international tale repertory, backed by much valuable interpretation, to the literature of ancient Greece.

The publication of *The Types of the Irish Folktale* (Ó Súilleabháin and Christiansen 1963) over a half century ago prepared the ground for comparatists to study what is arguably the richest oral tradition available in Western Europe. The Gaelic cultural area, as viewed by the eminent Irish folktale specialist James Delargy (1945, 29), comprises not only Ireland; it is part of a continuum that includes the traditions of Western Scotland. Until the eighteenth century, contacts in this region were constantly and methodically maintained at various levels of society, most notably among the professional learned orders. Delargy was aware as well of the prehistoric dimension, observing that:

...some of the wonder-tales alone contain unmistakable evidence of having belonged to a pre-Celtic civilization, perhaps pre-Indo-European. A number of these tales may have been told in Ireland in Megalithic times; indubitably, certain elements in them go back in Ireland at least as far as the Bronze Age. (Delargy 1945, 30)

But he pursued this direction no further. In fact, historical studies of folktales from Scotland and Ireland by scholars such as Alan Bruford (1969) and Kenneth Jackson (1936) have concentrated primarily on medieval sources. Medieval 'mythological' and other texts from Ireland - the earliest available - have attracted the attention of a number of comparatists such as Dumézil (1963), Puhvel (1987, 175-78) and Lyle (1990; 2012, 60-74). Considering the wealth of materials to draw on, such research is still in its initial stages.

By comparison with Ireland, less work is been done on the history of tales in Scotland. One collector remarkable in this regard, however, was the nineteenth-century Victorian polymath John Francis Campbell (1821-85). His publications of folktales, along with a vast legacy of papers left to the National Library of Scotland, provide abundant evidence from over a century and a half ago (and a good three to four generations before Delargy and Dumézil's time) of his interest in the larger questions of the geographical distribution and chronology of folktales. His collection, *Popular Tales of the West Highlands* first published in 1860-62, remains a standard work. In his lengthy introduction, he lays out on a grand scale his vision of the prehistory of tales he and his co-workers had collected in the Highlands:

> It is supposed that the race is known as Indo-European came from Central Asia at some very early period, and passed over Europe, separating and settling down as nations; retaining words of their original language, and leaving the traces of their religion and history everywhere as popular tales; and that they found the land occupied. Each wave, it is said, "pushed onwards those who went before," but, as it seems to me, each in turn must have stopped as it arrived at the great sea, and there the waves of the stream of men must have mingled and stagnated.

> As the flotsam and jetsam of American Rivers and of the Gulf Stream is constantly drifting northwards and eastwards, and finds a resting place on some western shore, so the traces of the great human stream, which is supposed to have flowed westwards, should be found in greatest abundance stranded at the western sea. (Campbell 1890, viii)

Campbell was a polyglot whose awareness of Indo-European philology and its applications to his own storytelling tradition was highly unusual for his time. Almost certainly, he had read and pondered the passage alluded to above in the 1856 edition of the Brothers Grimm collection.[1] During his later travels through North America, the Far East and South Asia, he made frequent mention of versions of tales encountered that he recognized, particularly one he termed the "Dragon Myth", now classified as ATU 300 (Campbell 1876). Of great interest for the study of the folktale in the nineteenth century is the manuscript of an unfinished work, "Oral Mythology", written (by his own account) during 1869-70, where he presents his views on the "science of storyology" at length.[2] His perspective owes much to developments in comparative philology, and many of the comparisons he draws incorporate Indic materials. In his attempts at applying the most modern methods to his own tradition, he reconstructs the *ur*-form of a story, "the restoration of a popular tale"; in his wider surveys, he employs the term 'comparative mythology' and discusses the various schools of the emerging discipline. He notes that tales have various levels of structure, likened to skeletons, which can be compared to each other through the practice of "comparative osteology", and observes that relations between folktale traditions seem to form a "net" between cultures. He then addresses such issues as the spatial distribution of tales, modes of transmission, and the question of monogenesis/polygenesis. These topics, observations and questions, along with Campbell's attempted answers, are still at the centre of comparative folktale research today.

TOWARD A LARGER COMPARATIVE CONTEXT

Recent advances in the study of the "deep"/pre- history of stories derive from larger sets of data available, more sophisticated systems of classification, and applications of advanced computer search technology. Prominent among these are the works of the Russian scholar Yuri Berezkin and the Sanskritist Michael Witzel, who, in the breadth of their comparative inquiries, have extended and superseded earlier studies conceived on a less ambitious scale. Such wider developments are a logical extension of the principles of the comparative method used for over two centuries in Indo-European language reconstruction (cf. Meillet 1954, 103 *et passim*), and more recently applied to other language groups. Inevitable questions have been raised concerning the application of language reconstruction techniques to higher levels of language such as traditional narrative, and particularly to the field of comparative mythology. But in many instances the similarities at this level between traditions are so close as to demand a consistent body of explanation.[3] In the past, studies within a more confined geographic area have been able to take us back, with whatever degree of accuracy, some 5000-6000 years at most. It is nevertheless evident that humanity was telling stories long before this, though no certain examples of narrative from this time have survived.

In more recent studies, researchers have therefore begun to explore wider sets of comparisons to achieve a greater time depth, applying essentially the same comparative technique used in the Folklore Fellows international tale monographs. The move toward opening up "wider, deeper" perspectives in folktale research has been in large part facilitated and supported by developments in the use of computer databases and population genetics.[4] Yuri Berezkin's research initially focussed on tracing the introduction of populations and their tales from the Asian continent to the Americas during the period(s) of prehistoric migration.[5] He has since extended this approach to western Eurasia and Africa, to gain a better understanding of prehistoric population movements and cultural contacts, and the "demographic and cultural processes which had place in prehistory and defined the global picture of the areal distribution of motifs" (nd. 1; 2007b, 70). At the centre of Berezkin's approach is a list of 1500 'motifs' (Electronic Catalogue of Folklore and Mythological Motifs; http://ruthenia.ru/folklore/berezkin/eng.htm), drawn from some 40,000 texts assembled from cultures worldwide (Berezkin 2007a, 4, 23; nd., 2). The occurrences of these motifs are entered into a database, articulated as an online map showing their geographical distribution. His 'motifs' are not to be taken as identical to those identified and listed by Stith Thompson; here they are more widely defined as 'any image, structure, element of the plot or any combination of such elements which could be found at least in two (practically, in many) texts', and are potentially infinite in number (2007b, 69-70). Berezkin observes that the new motifs contain some advantages for the comparatist, since 'their existence is not noticed by people who retell the texts' and thus can remain relatively stable in transmission (2007a, 3).[6]

In Berezkin's database, international folktales from both countries in the Gaelic cultural area, as listed in such catalogues as Aarne-Thompson and ATU, are entered, along with their global counterparts, since a good number of the motifs in his data correspond to international tale types, or entries in Thompson's motif index - though many others do not. The resources of the School of Scottish Studies folktale archive in Scotland provide an opportunity to contribute further to the database. This motivated me to undertake a preliminary survey in 2012, to see what more could "be found in greatest abundance stranded at the western sea", in John Francis Campbell's words. The survey was not intended to be exhaustive. The first step was to inspect the list of motifs in the online catalogue and mark those known at that stage to exist in Scottish tradition. These results were added to by consulting the list of ATU numbers given in Berezkin's database, corresponding to the motifs in the online Catalogue, and checking them against our own archive classification catalogue.[7] The next step was to compare the resulting items with the online geographical distribution map, keeping only those that were absent. The final list of motifs and, where appropriate, tale types known in Scotland but not listed by Berezkin, came to 17 tales.[8] In my discussion below of items selected from this list, and the questions arising regarding their origins, I have tried to remain aware of a number of caveats that have been incorporated into the online database. Important among these is the necessity of adhering precisely to the definition of the motif provided, and being aware that what can appear as a striking parallel may be due to an independent development (Berezkin 2007a, 4; 2007b, 81). Our discussion begins with items from our collection whose wider distribution appears to be fairly predictable, and proceeds to those whose profile is less so, or even anomalous. In all cases, items have been recorded or noted down in Scotland or in Gaelic-speaking Nova Scotia.

MOTIFS FROM SCOTLAND

L96. INTRICATE LEARNING (OH, DEAR!) = ATU 325 "THE MAGICIAN AND HIS PUPIL"

Demon teaches a youth to turn into animals. The youth has a narrow escape from the demon. Usually he returns home and asks his parent to sell him in guise of a horse, camel, etc., every time comes back. He warns not to sell his bridle. Demon buys animal with a bridle but the youth escapes again. Usually the story begins with the episode of a person saying, 'Oh, dear'; demon (named) emerges and gets person's son for a pupil to teach him magic".

Figure 1.
Motif code: 196
Name_eng: Sold in animal's guise and comes back
Description: Person can transform himself or herself into an animal
or an object. Being sold in this guise, he or she achieves his or her
aims and becomes a human again.

This is a well-known international tale, distributed throughout Eurasia
(Fig. 1), providing a good example of John Francis Campbell's theory of
the spread and diffusion of tales quoted above. Strongly represented in
Scotland with 17 recordings listed in the School of Scottish Studies
archive, together with numerous examples of the tale type in Ireland (Ó
Súilleabháin and Christiansen 1963).

H7A. Death and doctor = ATU 332 "Godfather Death" = D1825.3.1
"Magic power of seeing Death at head or foot of bed and thus
forecasting progress of sickness" [9]

Man receives from Death ability to see it near the bed of a patient
and understand will the patient die or recover. He becomes a rich
doctor because agrees to treat only those patients who will
certainly recover.

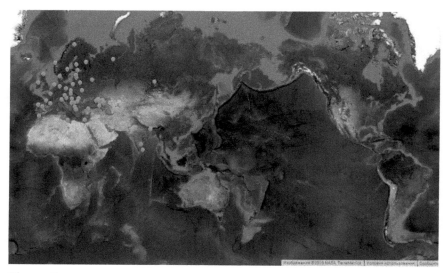

Figure 2.
Motif code: h7a
Name_eng: The Death and a doctor
Description: Man receives from Death (Fortune, some spirit)
knowledge will the patient recover or die. He becomes a doctor and
receives rich rewards. Usually he gets the ability to see Death near
the bed of a patient and considering a particular place where Death
stands, gets to know perspectives of recovering.

The Scottish variants, of which two have been recorded for the archive,
fall within a cluster whose main centre is in Europe (Fig. 2).

H7B. DEATH STICKS TO TREE = ATU 330 "THE SMITH AND THE DEVIL" =
Z111.2. "DEATH MAGICALLY BOUND TO TREE. WHILE HE IS BOUND NO ONE CAN
DIE".

    Person has an (apple)-tree, others cannot climb down from it
without his permission. He asks Death to climb this tree, Death is
stuck, for a long time nobody dies.

Figure 3.
Motif code: h7b
Name_eng: The Death in a tree
Description: A man has a tree from which nobody can climb down without his will. He lures there Death or Devil who came after him.

Five recordings in the archive.

A Gaelic variant, likely of Barra origin and recorded in Cape Breton, Nova Scotia begins with H7A followed by H7B (Shaw 2007, 68 – 73). Combining both units on the areal distribution website (Fig. 3) gives the following pattern, where we note the wide range of the two units combined (Fig. 4); the range and high-frequency of H7A alone; and the two only instances of H7B occurring alone, suggesting the possibility that the two units were originally combined and have remained closely associated.

Figure 4. h7A (Green) + H7B (Red) Combined (Yellow). Colours shown in Berezkin's database.

K64. ESCAPE FROM POLYPHEMOS' CAVE = ATU 1137 "THE BLINDED OGRE" = K521.1, K603.

Person gets into dwelling of master of animals or monstrous shepherd. The host can kill him. The hero escapes sticking to hair of one of the animals who are going out.

The Polyphemos story is routinely featured as an in-tale in Scottish Gaelic variants of ATU 953 "The Robber and His Sons" (Campbell 1890, 105-60; 1893, 314).

Well-established in Western Eurasia in a distribution similar to those we have seen above where Scotland fits in well (Fig. 5). However, its appearances in indigenous traditions in the western half of North America would indicate that its history extends back considerably to the time of the peopling of the Americas c. 14,000 BP (Berezkin 2007b, 67, 81, 83).

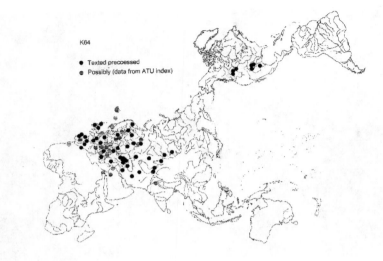

Figure 5: k64

J51. ONE PIECE IS MISSING.

Person or animal is eaten up or destroyed otherwise. His bones are put together and he or it is revived. Because one bone was broken, swallowed or lost, the person or animal cannot be revived or being revived misses some part of his or its body.

The motif (Fig. 6) appears in Scotland in the Gaelic story "The Battle of the Birds" (ATU 313 "The Magic Flight"), where the giant's daughter, in the course of helping the hero, loses her little finger. After their flight, she is identified by him from her missing finger (Campbell 1890, 25-63).

Figure 6.
Motif code: j51
Name_eng: One piece is missing
Description: Person or animal is eaten up or destroyed otherwise. His bones are out together and he or it is revived. Because one bone was broken, swallowed or lost, the person or animal cannot be revived or being revived misses from part of his or its body.

K66. EXTRAORDINARY COMPANIONS = ATU 513 "THE EXTRAORDINARY COMPANIONS" = F601 "EXTRAORDINARY COMPANIONS. A GROUP OF MEN WITH EXTRAORDINARY POWERS TRAVEL TOGETHER".

Several companions have extraordinary abilities (one who runs fast, one who eats great quantities, one who produces or can withstand severe frost, etc.)

This is the Argonauts' story, and is familiar to Scottish storytellers, with five recorded versions in the archive.
Its appearance in Europe, Asia, Africa, North America and the Pacific (Fig. 7) suggests a long life for the motif in prehistoric times.

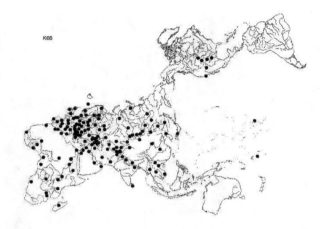

Figure 7. k66

L15D. LIFE PRESERVED OUTSIDE OF THE BODY = E710 EXTERNAL SOUL. A
PERSON (OFTEN A GIANT OR OGRE) KEEPS HIS SOUL OR LIFE SEPARATE FROM THE
REST OF HIS BODY.

Life of a person or creature is preserved outside of his body. He
dies after the corresponding object is destroyed.

In Scotland, as in other cultures, the motif is associated with ATU 302
"The Ogre's (Devil's) Heart in an Egg". It is found in three tale summaries
in the archive, and in printed collections from nineteenth century collectors
(McKay 1940, 2-47; D. MacInnes 1890, 94-113; Campbell 1890, 1-24;
MacDougall 1891, 76-144). It is plentiful in Europe, and its wide
distribution (Fig. 8) suggests it may have been present at an early stage
in human migration. The concept of the external soul is present elsewhere
in Scotland's Gaelic traditions. The Gaelic expression *thilg e amach
'anam,* 'he expelled his soul' is associated with the act of dying. In Gaelic
song tradition, from as far back as the sixteenth century, there are allusions
in a half dozen songs to women drinking their lover's blood at the time
of death, as an act of mourning (John MacInnes 2010, 325). There is
some linguistic evidence as well from Old Irish: the literal meaning of
the verb *at-bail(l)* 'dies' is 'he throws it', from an ancient verbal root:
Gk bállō < IE *gwelh- "throw, hurl".

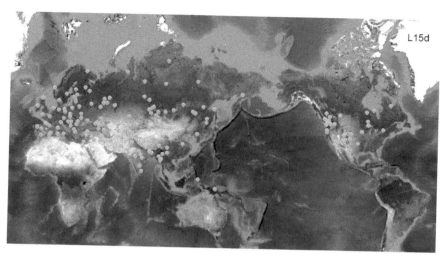

Figure 8. 115D

The final group of motifs I selected for discussion primarily because their appearance in Scotland relative to those provided on the map is surprising; with the possible exception of K91, if judged to be genuine, our versions would be isolates within Europe.

I7A. LIGHTNING-SERPENT.

Lightning is associated with snake.

Linguistic evidence suggests an earlier association of this kind in Scotland. Curiously, Gael. *beithir* 'lightning, thunderbolt' also means 'serpent', although the link may well occur independently due to visual similarities (Fig. 9).

Figure 9.
Motif code: i7a
Name_eng: The lightning-serpent
Description: the lightning is associated with a snake.

K91. INVISIBLE BATTLE.

Hero's dogs or horse (rare: he himself) fight with his adversary in the lower world, under the water. Those who are on the bank get to know about the outcome of the combat according to the color of water or foam that rises to the surface.

I give here the medieval version because of its exceptional interest as an isolate in Europe, if indeed it belongs to the motif as described in the Catalogue (Fig. 10).[10] The oldest and most extensive version is *Echtra Fergusa maic Léti,* 'The Saga of Fergus mac Léti' found in a medieval Irish law text. The translation runs:

> One day he told his bondmaid to wash his head. Thinking that the woman was too slow in carrying out this, he gave her a blow with his whip. Resentment overcame her and she taunted him to his

t

Figure 10.
Motif code: k91
Name_eng: An invisible battle
Description: Hero's dogs or horse or (rare) he himself fight with his adversary in the underworld (under the water). Those who are waiting for the outcome of the combat understand who overcomes whom by the colour of water or foam that rises to the surface.

face with his blemish. He gave her a blow with his sword and cut her in two. Thereupon he turned away and went under Loch Rudraige; for a whole day and night the loch seethed from [the contest between] him and the muirdris, and the surge of its waves kept coming on to the land. Eventually he emerged on the surface of the loch, holding the head of the monster, so that the Ulaid saw him, and he said to them: 'I am the survivor.' Thereupon he sank down dead, and for a whole month the loch remained red from [the battle between] them. (Binchy 1952, 43-4)

The parallel is not perfect: I have found no Irish versions yet where the onlookers do actually 'get to know' the outcome of the struggle under the surface from the colour of the water. However, a second variant printed in *Silva Gadelica* (from Eg. 1782, fol. 30B col. 1) provides some

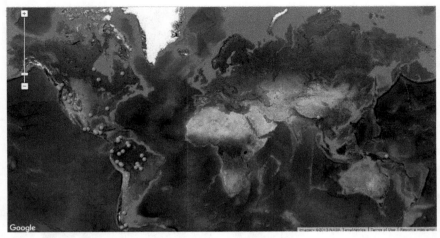

Figure 11. j1

Now was the loch whiter than new milk, anon all turned to crimson froth of blood (O'Grady, 251)

There is the practical question as to how spectators could be expected to perceive the outcome before at least one of the adversaries breaks the surface, blood or no blood, and we should note the two colours mentioned, along with the direct reference to 'foam' (*cubar*). Watkins (1995, 441-47) views the Irish story as being of considerable antiquity, derived from a widely distributed Indo-European dragon-slayer myth.

J1. VENGEFUL HEROES = H1228. QUEST UNDERTAKEN BY HERO FOR VENGEANCE.

MacInnes describes this as follows: "A cycle of tales widely known across Central and South America, losing some typical traits in North America and Europe and practically absent as a coherent unit in other areas [cf. Fig. 11]. Standard plot: 'Victim is killed by Antagonist; Hero is grown up by Adoptive Parent (if Hero's father was killed, the functions of Adoptive Parent can be fulfilled by his biological mother); Messenger (usually small animal or bird, sometimes the spirit of the killed parent) tells Hero about his origins; Hero kills Antagonist and sometimes meets afterwards Protector. In many versions, Adoptive Parent is also killed that can be motivated by his or her relation (either close or uncertain and distant) to Antagonist. Adoptive Parent's characteristics easily vary [through the spectrum] between Antagonist and Protector." MacInnes (2010, 59-60)

Gaels in the Hebrides are familiar from their clan saga traditions with tales of vengeance following the pattern outlined above and described by MacInnes, where the young hero (often as an infant), because of internecine strife, is forced to flee his native territory, sometimes accompanied by his mother, to be nurtured on the outside and return as a grown man to exact revenge.

I19. People inhale odor of food/The Steam Eaters (cf. Berezkin 2007b, 279).

Anthropomorphic beings satisfy their hunger cooking food and inhaling the odo[u]r. (see Fig. 12)

In 1692, Robert Kirk, Minister of Aberfoyle in the southern Highlands, published a lengthy treatise on fairies, their physical nature, dwellings and habits, based on local traditions he had noted down. The fairies are described at some length: they would seem to be at the very least exotic when compared to the modern layman's conceptions of these legendary beings. Nevertheless, a detailed comparison of the fairy lore from the Perthshire minister against the extensive catalogue of fairy legends compiled in the School archive (MacDonald 1994-5, 43-78) reveals a clear majority of Kirk's items confirmed by folk traditions recorded during the twentieth-century. That the 'Lychnobious people' of Kirk's account are anthropomorphic there can be no doubt, for they dress and speak much like locals:

Figure 12.
Motif code: i19
Name_eng: People inhale the odour of food
Description: Anthropomorphic beings satisfy their hunger cooking
food and inhaling the odour.

Their apparell and speech is like that of the people and countrey
under which they live: so are they seen to wear plaids and
variegated garments in the high-lands of Scotland and Suanochs
heretofore in Ireland. They speak but litle, and that by way of
whistling, clear, not rough: the verie devils conjured in any
Countrey, doe answer in the Language of the place: yet sometimes
these Subterraneans speak more distinctly then at other times.
(Kirk, in Hunter 2001, 82)

As for their sustenance, they are not above abstracting food 'by secret
paths' from sources removed, or the essence of milk from surrounding
settlements:

Some have bodies or vehicles so spungious, thin and defecate
[delicate?]: that they are fed by only sucking into some fine
spirituous liquor (that pierce like pure air and oyl): others feed

more gross on the foyson or substance of cornes and liquors, or on corn itselfe, that grows on the surface of the Earth; which these fairies steall away, partly invisible, partly preying on the grain as do Crows and Mice. Wherfore (in this Sam age) they are somtimes heard to bake bread, strike hammers, and to do such (like) services within the litle hillocks where they (most) haunt... (79)

The best of Spirits having alwayes delighted more to appear into aereal, then into Terrestrial Body's. They feed most what on quintessences, and Ethereal Essences: the pith and spirits only of Womens milk feed their Children, being artificially convey'd (as air and oyl sink into our Bodys) to make them vigorous and fresh. And this shorter way of conveying a pure Aliment (without the usual digestions) by transfusing it, and transpyring thorow the pores into the veins and arteries, and vessells that supply the body, is nothing more absurd, than an Infants being fed by the Navel before it is borne ... (103)

CONCLUSION

Whether the above correspondences between items of Scottish tradition and the motifs listed in the online Electronic Catalogue of Folklore and Mythological Motifs are appropriate for global study involving oral traditions of *longue durée*, or are more likely attributable to an imprecise formulations or independent origins, is a question to be asked whenever archives are consulted as a point of departure for exploring the prehistory of traditions. Pending further research from scholars familiar with the wider extent of the motifs in the Catalogue, we cannot with certainty propose an interpretation of the significance of those from Scotland examined here. It is, however, worth noting interpretations that have been published concerning similar motif distributions, and what they may reveal of migrations of peoples and traditions. Items found in Eurasia and the Americas have origins at least as far back as the population movements in that direction, as in the case of the Polyphemos motif. We cannot at present say, however, at what point the motif became part of the tale repertoire in Scotland. According to the model proposed by Witzel (2012, 4-5, 64-104), items recorded throughout Eurasia and extending with migrations into the Americas form a coherent body of 'myth traditions', termed 'Laurasian', that originated some 40,000 years ago, and extended with migrations to the Americas, eventually embracing a territory from Iceland to Tierra del Fuego. Some items securely represented in Africa may belong to the oldest layer of motifs known, and be at least as ancient as the time of early eastward migration from that continent into Eurasia (Berezkin 2007a, 1ff.).

The list from which I have drawn our selections from Scottish tradition is by necessity provisional, and all items are subject to a careful comparison with the source materials of variants on the database currently not available to me, before they can be confirmed and accepted into the wider resource. Also, we should bear in mind that my examination covers only a minute percentage of items in Scottish folktales worthy of consideration. Further sources would include the wealth of items available in the *numerous Scottish folktale publications from the nineteenth to the twenty-first centuries*, both Gaelic and Scots; the hundreds of unpublished tales in the manuscript collections of the National Library of Scotland from nineteenth century collectors such as John Francis Campbell and Alexander Carmichael; and the hundreds of tales recorded in the twentieth century and available online in the Calum Maclean collection database (www.calum-maclean-project.celtscot.ed.ac.uk*)*, including the Thompson international motif numbers provided there. The results of such a study, combined with those of a parallel initiative for tales published and recorded from Irish tradition, would provide a representation that, once integrated with the online Catalogue, would reveal much concerning the "deep history" of the folktales that arrived on this "western shore."

John Shaw is an Honorary Fellow in the Department of Celtic and Scottish Studies, University of Edinburgh.

Notes

1   His copy of the relevant volume (3) containing the passage is among his books now held at the National Library of Scotland (NLS).

2   NLS Adv. MS 50.3.2.

3   John Colarusso (1998) examines the probability model underlying comparative linguistics, and how it applies to comparative mythology. See also Witzel's (2012, 51) table of 'Parallels between linguistics and

mythology'.

4   It also 'opens the possibility to claim back the legacy of the Finnish school' (Berezkin 2007b, 69).

5   He is not the first to study the passage of narratives over this migration route, as evidenced by the earlier work of Utley (1974) and Boas.

6   Cf. Colarusso's observation (1998, 103) regarding the work of Dumézil that "the examination of such precise detail is in fact the fundamental principle on which all comparative work rests."

7   The survey was based primarily on items in our folktale catalogue corresponding to the ATU classification numbers associated with the motifs in Berezkin's online Catalogue. Added to this were items known to the writer from printed sources and field recordings.

8   Since 2012 some of the motifs on the list have been included in the database, when regarded as appropriate. Originally two lists were sent to Berezkin: the first based on motifs listed in the Catalogue; the second on ATU classification numbers, since the map distributions for motifs and ATU international tales did not always correspond exactly.

9   Where applicable, numbers from Thompson's Motif-index are included here and below.

10 An oral version in Scottish Gaelic does exist, recorded in the field some 30 years ago from a Gaelic speaker in Cape Breton, Nova Scotia, but is almost certainly a secondary one based on a book version in English and re-oralised by storytellers locally.

References & Further Reading

Berezkin, Yuri E. 2010. "The Emergence of the First People from the Underworld: Another Cosmogonic Myth of a Possible African Origin." In *New Perspectives on Myth. Proceedings of the Second Annual Conference of the International Association for Comparative Mythology. Ravenstein (the Netherlands), 19-21 August, 2008*, edited by Wim M. J. Binsbergen and Eric Venbrux, 109–125. PIP-TraCS: Papers in Intercultural Philosophy and Transcontinental Comparative Studies 5. Haarlem: Shikanda.

Berezkin, Yuri E. 2007a. "Out of Africa and Further Along the Coast: African-South Asian-Australian Mythological Parallels." *Cosmos* 23:3-28.

_____ 2007b. "Dwarfs and cranes. Baltic Finnish mythologies in Eurasian and American perspective (70 years after Yrio Toivonen)." *Folklore* 36:75-96.

Binchy, D. A. 1952. "The Saga of Fergus Mac Léti." In *Contributions in Memory of Osborn Bergin*, special issue, *Ériu* 16:33-48.

Bruford, Alan. 1969. *Gaelic Folk-Tales and Medieval Romances*. Dublin: The Folklore of Ireland Society.

Campbell, John Francis. 1890-3 [1860-2]. *Popular Tales of the West Highlands*. 2nd ed. 4 vols. Reprint. Detroit: Singing Tree Press 1969.

_____ 1876. *My circular notes. Extracts from journals, letters sent home, geological and other notes, written while travelling westwards round the world, from July 6, 1874, to July 6, 1875*. New York: Macmillan.

Christiansen, R.T. 1927. "A Gaelic Fairytale in Norway." *Béaloideas* 1:107-14.

Colarusso, John. 1998. "Dumézil and the Details: An Analysis of the Comparative Technique in Linguistics and Mythology." *Cosmos* 14:103-17.

Delargy, James. 1945. "The Gaelic Storyteller." In *Proceedings of the British Academy*, vol. 31, 1-47. Oxford: Oxford University Press.

Dumézil, Georges. 1963. "Le puits de Nechtan." *Celtica* 6:50-61.

Hansen, William. 2002. *Ariadne's Thread*. Ithaca and London: Cornell University Press.

Hunter, Michael. 2001. *The Occult Laboratory. Magic, Science and Second Sight in Late Seventeenth-Century Scotland. A new edition of Robert Kirk's The Secret Commonwealth and other texts*. Woodbridge: The Boydell Press.

Jackson, Kenneth. 1936. "The International Folktale in Ireland." *Folk-Lore* 47:263–93.

Jason, Heda. 1981. "How Old Are Folktales?" *Fabula* 22:1-27.

Lyle, Emily. 1990. *Archaic Cosmos*. Edinburgh: Polygon.

_____ 2012. *Ten Gods. A New Approach to Defining the Mythological Structures of the Indo- Europeans*. Newcastle: Cambridge Scholars Publishing.

MacDonald, Donald Archie. 1994-5. "Migratory Legends of the Supernatural in Scotland: A General Survey." *Béaloideas* 62-63, 29-78.

MacDougall, J. 1891. *Folk and Hero Tales*. London: The Folklore Society.

MacInnes, D. 1890. *Folk and Hero Tales*. London: The Folklore Society.

MacInnes, John and Michael Newton, ed. 2010. *Dùthchas nan Gàidheal. Selected Essays of John MacInnes*. Edinburgh: Birlinn.

McKay, J.G. 1940. *More West Highland Tales.* Edinburgh and London: Oliver and Boyd.

Meillet, Antoine. 1954. *La méthode comparative en linguistique historique.* Paris: Librarie Ancienne Honoré Champion.

O'Grady, Standish Hayes. 1892. *Silva Gadelica.* London: Williams and Norgate.

Ó Súilleabháin, Seán and Christiansen, Reidar Th. 1963. *The Types of the Irish Folktale.* Helsinki: Folklore Fellows Communications.

Puhvel, Jaan. 1987. *Comparative Mythology.* Baltimore and London: The Johns Hopkins University Press.

Shaw, John. 2007. *The Blue Mountains and Other Gaelic Stories from Cape Breton/Na Beanntaichean Gorma agus Sgeulachdan Eile à Ceap Breatainn.* Montreal: McGill-Queen's University Press.

Thompson, Stith. 1955-58. *Motif-index of Folk Literature.* 6 vols. Bloomington:Indiana University Press.

Utley, Francis Lee. 1974. "The Migration of Folktales: Four Channels to the Americas." *Current Anthropology* 15:5-13.

Uther, Hans-Jörg. 2004. *The Types of International Folktale. A Classification and Bibliography.* FF Communications 284. 3 vols. Helsinki: Suomalainen tiedeakatemia.

The Return of the Oppressed: Intra-Social Inequality and Supernatural Agency in the Táin and Crofton Croker's "Teigue of the Lee"

JAMES CARNEY

Department of Psychology, Lancaster University

ABSTRACT. *The Curse of Macha episode from Táin Bó Cuailgne and Thomas Crofton Croker's "Teigue of the Lee" display remarkable similarities, despite being separated by several centuries and coming from very different cultural milieu. A typical explanation for this would centre on historical transmission; here, I suggest that a more plausible account is delivered by cognitive science. Specifically, the 'fear of supernatural punishment' hypothesis argues that there is a cross-cultural tendency to identify supernatural beings as morally concerned, omnipresent punitive agents. My claim is that the two relevant texts can be thought of as attempts to refract historically specific social inequalities using this universal cognitive frame. The value of this position is that it delivers new interpretations of its target texts while showcasing the usefulness of placing cognitive science in the service of cultural analysis.*

KEYWORDS: *Teigue of the Lee, Curse of Macha, supernatural punishment, cognitive historical approach.*

INTRODUCTION

For several years now, the study of cultural materials has benefited from the insights of cognitive science. To cite only a small selection, contributions have been made to the understanding of Greek music (Budelmann and LeVen 2014), Anglo-Saxon poetics (Harbus 2012), Roman horticulture (Jones 2014), English medieval hagiography (Farina 2012), narrative fiction (Zunshine 2006), Old French *chansons de geste* (Leverage 2010), comic-book literature (Carney et al. 2014) and Celtic religion (Sjöblom 2000). Implicit in these interventions (and those like them) is the idea that the human cultural endowment is not exhausted by its historical determinations; instead, they propose that it emerges by way of a two-way interaction between innate tendencies in human cognition and contingent forms of historical experience. Variously characterised as 'cognitive historicism' (Spolsky 2003) or 'semiotic scaffolding' (Cobley and Stjernfelt 2015), this type of approach has done a great deal to mitigate the effects of both heavy-handed psychologism and historicist reductionism in the study of cultural and generic traditions.

In the present article, I contribute to this literature by using a cognitive perspective to compare two Irish narratives from legendary and folkloric sources. Specifically, my goal is to show that the Curse of Macha pre-narrative to *Táin Bó Cuailgne* and Thomas Crofton Croker's "Teigue of the Lee" derive their structure from the same set of innate intuitions linking supernatural animation to moral violations. These latter intuitions I exposit in the context of the 'fear of supernatural punishment hypothesis,' which is a position in the cognitive anthropology of religion that seeks to explain the cross-cultural belief in the existence of counterfactual beings like gods, spirits and ghosts (Piazza, Bering, and Ingram 2011; Johnson and Krüger 2004). My purpose in making these connections is twofold. On the one hand, by engaging with two thematically similar narratives between which there could have been no direct transmission of influence, I hope to show how knowledge of human cognition can play a role in explaining otherwise inexplicable commonalities between texts. On the other, exploring the very different situations of these texts allows me to illustrate how historical context nuances the expression of very coarse grained cross-cultural psychological dispositions. If successful, these undertakings should advance our understanding of the two texts from the insular Celtic tradition, both in terms of their relation to each other and to the generic features of the human mind. Equally, they should illustrate the value of the cognitive historical approach, in which "the evolved human mind itself is folded into the investigation of the processes of cultural construction, complicating but also enriching the discussion" (Spolsky 2003, 168).

At a practical level, I begin with an exposition of the fear of supernatural punishment hypothesis, with a view to showing the empirical grounds for the claims that I shall make here. Once I have done this, I shall deliver accounts of the Curse of Macha narrative and "Teigue of the Lee" through the lens of this hypothesis. Ideally, this should provide grounds for my basic contention that each text represents the same cognitive intuition, refracted through very different historical circumstances.

THE FEAR OF SUPERNATURAL PUNISHMENT HYPOTHESIS (FSPH)

Every culture on record exhibits a belief in counterfactual agents in the form of supernatural or paranatural beings (Boyer 2001, 2003). Given that these beliefs are both unverifiable and costly, they pose something of a puzzle in the study of culture. After all, why go to the trouble of acquiring, maintaining and publicising a set of counterfactual beliefs when it would be far easier to forego them entirely? And yet, even among individuals who explicitly disavow such beliefs, supernatural and quasi-supernatural ideas recur with surprising frequency (Pereira, Faísca, and de Sá-Saraiva 2012; Raman and Winer 2004; Baumard and Chevallier 2012). Thus, their questionable epistemic status notwithstanding, it would seem reasonable to conclude that a belief in counterfactual agents confers an advantage on those who profess it.

Though there is no consensus on what this advantage might be, one influential approach maintains that the belief in supernatural agents persists because it fosters social solidarity. There are many versions of this hypothesis, but the one of interest here is sometimes termed the 'fear of supernatural punishment hypothesis' (FSPH); it claims that the traits typically assigned to supernatural agents play a causal role in disincentivising defections from social norms. This idea starts with recognising that the presence of a witness makes agents unwilling to engage in antisocial behaviour (Bateson, Nettle, and Roberts 2006). First, this is because the witness may have a stake in the norm being preserved, and is thus likely to engage in counteraction when it is broken. Second, even in cases where the witness is not directly disadvantaged by norm breaking, there is a large body of evidence showing that humans (and even apes) are willing to engage in third-party enforcement of social norms (Fehr and Fischbacher 2004; Henrich et al. 2006; Flack et al. 2006; Bendor and Swistak 2001). Necessarily, this leaves those scenarios in which there are *no* witnesses open to exploitation—and here is where supernatural agents enter the picture. Clearly, a belief that *all* actions are witnessed by invisible agents capable of engaging in punitive action would provide a permanent disincentive against wrongdoing, thereby protecting individuals from the consequences of breaking social norms when they might otherwise be tempted to do so (Johnson 2015; Norenzayan 2013). To this extent, a tendency to believe in all-seeing, invisible and morally concerned supernatural agents would have conferred important benefits that may well have outweighed the cost of supporting such beliefs. In the words of Quentin Atkinson and Pierrick Bourrat:

The threat of supernatural punishment (in this life or the afterlife) arising from belief in morally concerned supernatural agents can help enforce cooperative norms by exporting the cost of enforcement to ostensibly infallible supernatural forces beyond the group. Belief in a punitive supernatural agent can, in principle, exert this effect without requiring that the imagined agent actually punishes free riders—it is enough that group members perceive such a threat. (2011, 42)

The question all of this poses is whether the experimental and ethnographic evidence actually corroborates the FSPH. In the former area, experimental interventions support the view that there is an association between supernatural agency and punitive animation (Piazza, Bering, and Ingram 2011; Bering, McLeod, and Shackelford 2005). The 'Princess Alice' experiment performed by Piazza et al (2011) is instructive in this regard. Here, groups of children were exposed to cheating opportunities in three scenarios: when they were primed to believe that an empty chair contained an invisible agent, 'Princess Alice'; when an actual adult supervised; and when they were entirely unsupervised. Results showed that, for children who believed in the presence of Princess Alice, cheating was deterred to the same degree as it was by the presence of a real adult—a clear endorsement of the FSPH. Ethnographically, there is also substantial evidence for a cross-cultural belief in punitive supernatural agents. Surveys by Bering and Johnson (2005), Atkinson and Bourrat (2011), Bourrat, Atkinson and Dunbar (2011), Johnson (2005), Johnson (2015) and Johnson and Krüger (2004) all identify a propensity to act "as if our thoughts and actions will be judged, if not by God, then by some other cosmic, karmic, or supernatural force" (Johnson 2015, 6). Indeed, homely examples can be found in contemporary children's culture, where figures like Santa Claus and the comic-book superhero, as well as practices like trick-or-treating, identify supernatural or quasi-supernatural agency with the capacity to punish anti-social behaviour.

Thus, there is good evidence to support the presence of the FSPH as a staple of human psychology. To be sure, this does not imply that all forms of putative supernatural agency can be explained by the FSPH, or that the FSPH is the only constraint operating on human moral behaviour. Nevertheless, it does point to the value of the FSPH when it comes to engaging with textual representations of supernatural or quasi-supernatural agency—a line of inquiry that has already been pursued to good effect by the present author and others (Carney et al. 2014; Carney 2014; Boyd

2009; Carney 2007). In the following sections, I extend the FSPH to the Curse of Macha episode and "Teigue of the Lee," and show how both texts use the FSPH to interrogate norm violations in the form of inegalitarian social relationships.

TÁIN BÓ CUAILGNE AND THE FSPH

Though the survival of the Irish epic *Táin Bó Cuailgne* in three recensions presents the usual difficulties of extracting a consistent narrative (Dooley 2006), the division of the action into the *Táin* proper and *rémscela* (or pre-narratives) is generally accepted. These latter consist of short narrative vignettes that explain how the various situations that bear on the action of the *Táin* came about. Moreover, their purpose is not entirely expository: as I show in Carney (2008), different *rémscela* can be conceived of as semantic inverses of each other. Here, I indicate how one *rémscel* in particular (the Curse of Macha episode) can be understood using the FSPH—and in this way relate the supernatural elements of the text to the exploitative social relationship it documents.

First, it is useful to recall the details. The narrative recounts how a rich peasant, Crunnchu son of Agnoman, took a new wife, Macha, of likely supernatural origin, after his first wife died. Macha gifted her husband with prosperity and fertility, asking him only not to attend fair day when the time came close. He insisted on going regardless, so she compromised by making him promise not to mention her. On the day, Crunnchu attended the races and witnessed the king's horses win several times. Forgetting himself, he boasted that his wife could outrace they royal horses were she present. Hearing this, the king immediately demanded that she be brought in front of him. Macha, who was pregnant with twins, begged leave to deliver her children before being forced to race. She was refused, and at that cursed nine generations of Ulstermen to suffer the pangs of a pregnant woman for five days and four nights whenever they faced grave danger. In the event, Macha defeated the king's horses, but, on the finish line, she gave a great cry and was delivered of her twins. Ever since, the capital of the Ulaid (Ulstermen) was known as Emain Macha, or Macha's fort.

Viewing this narrative through the lens of the FSPH, it is evident that all the relevant features are in place. There is a supernatural agent (Macha), a violated social norm (the exploitation of a pregnant woman) and a punitive response (Macha's curse). However, matters runs a little deeper than this. As one of the three Machas of the insular Celtic tradition,

Macha is not just an arbitrary representative of the class of supernatural beings: she is, in fact, a fertility goddess, whose exploitation symbolically enacts the primal act of subordination by which sovereignty is established (Mac Cana 1983, 88). This can be read topographically as the conquest of the land that comprises the kingdom; a more plausible interpretation might focus on the ongoing subordination of the subject populations and their productive capacities. On this reading, Macha's travails represent an act of appropriation, in which her curse expresses the intra-social antagonism that emerges from the oppression of one class by another.

How plausible is this reading? Outside of the *Táin*, the wider Indo-European mythological and legendary record offers numerous parallels to this scenario by way of what is sometimes termed 'the war of the foundation' (Mallory 1997, 1989). This motif centres on a primordial war in which the martial and juridical classes of society combine with the class of agrarian producers, either by way of military victory or negotiated compromise. Relevant examples from myth and legend include the conflict between the Aesir and the Vanir in Scandinavian myth (Dumézil 1973), the rape of the Sabines in Roman pseudo-history (Momigliano 1987), the Graeco-Trojan conflict in Homeric literature (Littleton 1970) and the first battle of Mag Tuired between the Túatha Dé Danaan and the Formorians in the Irish *Book of Invasions* (O'Brien 1997). Possible historical instances include the ephors' annual declaration of war against the helots in Spartan society (de Ste Croix 1981), as well as the 'apartheid' that, on genetic evidence, may have been practised against the indigenous Britons in Anglo-Saxon England (Thomas, Stumpf, and Härke 2006). What all of these parallels suggest is that the Curse of Macha is an Irish reflection of a foundational narrative that accounts for inegalitarian social arrangements across the Indo-European cultural area.

For all that, contextual evidence of this sort remains circumstantial in the absence of any direct connection with the text. Happily, internal evidence for this sociological interpretation emerges when the Curse of Macha is compared with the other *rémscela*. As I have made this comparison at length in Carney (2008), I not repeat the exercise here, except to note its general features. The central point is that both the Naming of Cú Chulainn and the Curse of Macha *rémscela* can be seen as semantic inverses of each other. That is, just as the Curse of Macha documents a violation of solidarity between classes, the Naming of Cú Chulainn announces the restoration of the same solidarity. This follows because Cú Chulainn's assuming of his warrior identity centres on his defence of the household of Culann, the blacksmith, after he has killed the fearsome hound that formerly performed this duty ('Cú Chulainn' =

	CURSE OF MACHA	NAMING OF CÚ CHULAINN
LOCATION	A fair	A feast
PARTICIPANTS	King, warriors, peasants	King, warriors, artisan
INJUNCTION	Macha not to be mentioned	Setanta not to be forgotten
CONSEQUENCE OF BREAKING INJUNCTION	Macha raced against king's horses	Setanta pitted against fearsome hound
RESULT	Fertility themed curse delivered by Macha	Fertility themed theft prevented by Cú Chulainn
NATURE OF SOCIAL CHARTER ESTABLISHED	Negative reciprocity between classes	Positive reciprocity between classes

Table 1. Correspondences between the Curse of Macha and the Naming of Cú Chulainn *rémscela*

'the hound of Culann'). In this way, Cú Chulainn and Culann can be viewed as homologous with the Ulster nobles and Macha in the Curse of Macha episode—a homology supported by several other correspondences in both narratives (see Table 1). The *significance* of the inverted parallel is that it is quite unlikely that a negative concordance of this type would be present unless the identified dynamic were present in both *rémscela*. Thus, the principles of selection (or creation) that prefaced the *Táin* with the relevant *rémscela* were not arbitrary, but instead concerned with exploring the twin acts of contracting and violating social reciprocity.

Relating all of this back to the FSPH, what emerges is that the *rémscela* to the *Táin* use inherited intuitions about morality and supernatural agency to explore inegalitarian social relationships. This is not done in the form of a simplistic substitution, where cultural tokens are moved about in accordance with the script of a pre-existing psychodrama. Instead, the authors of the relevant *rémscela* consciously amplify and shape their raw material, both in relation to an existing tradition and to their local historical situation. Thus, though the FSPH provides a cosmological frame for the Curse of Macha episode, it does so at an extremely high level of generality; the specific content of the episode can only be understood by way of comparative or historical investigation. Unfortunately, the paucity of reliable historical material from the first century CE in Ireland means that such reconstructions must retain a speculative character—not, it should be said, that there is no value in pursuing them. As this lack of evidence is emphatically not the case for the second narrative I wish to analyse—Crofton Croker's "Teigue of the Lee"—I now move on to discuss how the FSPH manifests itself in a more modern context.

"TEIGUE OF THE LEE" AND THE FSPH

The work of Thomas Crofton Croker sits uneasily in the enterprise of Irish folkloristics. On the one hand, his three-volume *Fairy Legends and Traditions of the South of Ireland* (1828) offers a timely selection from the folk tradition before it was decimated by the potato famine of the 1840s. To this extent, Crofton Croker—with figures like Standish O'Grady and Samuel Ferguson—played a vital role in compiling the materials that later provided the basis for the Irish Cultural Revival. On the other hand, the deracinated whimsy of Crofton Croker's narratives speaks less of ethnographic rigour than it does of cultural myopia on the part of this Anglo-Irish Protestant Ascendency writer. In the words of B.G. MacCarthy, Crofton Croker "belonged to a garrison as truly cut off from the real life of Ireland as if, in fact, they were enclosed within the Pale" (1943, 541)—an assessment entirely consonant with the tone-deaf liberties Crofton Croker took with his source material.

Though his equivocations complicate any attempt to analyse Crofton Croker's narratives as folkloric artefacts, I here deliver, using the FSPH, a reading of his "Teigue of the Lee" that identifies it as an allegory of social unrest. Though by no means the most popular of the stories from the 1828 collection—it was easily eclipsed by "Daniel O'Rourke"— "Teigue of the Lee" nevertheless presents several points of interest that go beyond its surface content. This latter fact is important, given that the surface content does not, at first glance, seem to offer an awful lot. The story is a somewhat bloodless account of an escapade involving the eponymous Teigue, a type of *genius loci* inhabiting Carrigrohane manor house in Cork, and a Colonel Pratt. It begins with a dinner, where the invisible Teigue embarrasses various guests and servants by revealing their peccadilloes, pretensions and minor moral infractions. Enraged, Colonel Pratt, the brother of the manor's owner, resolves to make Teigue pay for such impudence. Teigue continues to goad him, making him give chase, and leading him by degrees to Hell-hole, a deep pool in the nearby river Lee. The colonel hears Teigue jump into the pool, and returns to Carrigrohane House—only to find Teigue there ahead of him. Teigue then demands and receives dinner, consuming it only when the company agree to look away.

Much as the Curse of Macha in the *Táin* can be interpreted as expressing intra-social antagonism, I hold here that the supernatural animation associated with Teigue betokens a similar breakdown in solidarity. As might be expected from historical context, I locate this breakdown in the consequences of the 1801 Act of Union between Great Britain and Ireland, and the agrarian violence that accompanied it. That is, I volunteer the character of Teigue as an encoding, using the logic of the FSPH, of those restitutive secret societies who defended Catholic tenant farmers from exploitation by landlords. Before discussing the historical dimension to this claim, I first examine the supernatural aspect to the representation of Teigue, which is crucial to understanding how this history is framed.

It is notable that Teigue is not, in fact, a spirit. This possibility is discounted early on in the text due to Teigue being active during the day; equally, Teigue's propensity for whiskey drinking and fine dining points to a decidedly material digestive process. Crofton Croker, for his part, identifies Teigue as a 'fir darrig' (*fear dearg*) or 'red man'—a class of beings in Irish folklore associated with low-key mischief. W.B. Yeats, when anthologising "Teigue of the Lee" in his 1892 *Irish Fairy Tales*, makes a similar attribution, classifying Teigue under the category of 'Land and Water Fairies.' To this extent, Teigue belongs, however distantly, to the same class of beings as Macha. With respect to Teigue's specific capacities, he has a typically supernatural ability to negotiate any spatial or physical barrier, and his most important feature for present discussion must be the moral omniscience he evinces. He reminds the servant, John Sheehan, of the time he stole spoons from a former master; another guest, Mr Bell, when he takes a glass of wine, is pricked about his forgotten Quaker heritage; the *nouveau-riche* Mr Parkes is mocked for his fashionable affectations; the exciseman Mr Cole is prodded for drinking alcohol. Teigue's particular target, however, is Colonel Pratt, "the biggest dust of them all" (1828, 276)—presumably in relation to activities in the Indies, which Teigue takes care to mention as his station.

Viewing all of this through the lens of the FSPH, Teigue thus seems to satisfy the notion that supernatural agents "function as moral big brothers who keep a constant vigil to dissuade would-be cheaters and free riders" (Atran 2002, 112).

And yet, the identification remains unsatisfying. For all that Teigue may be a punitive supernatural watcher, no one is guilty of anything significant and no one is actually punished—thereby making the whole supernatural infrastructure of the text redundant. For sure, this may be due to Crofton Croker's mishandling of his materials, which Yeats (with justice) represented as reducing the *aos sí* to "dancing mannikins" and "buffoons of the darkness" (1891, 5). However, the historical setting of the narrative suggests an alternative hypothesis: Teigue is a representation of agrarian and Catholic secret societies like the Whiteboys, the Levellers and the Ribbonmen, who, in the late eighteenth and early nineteenth centuries, violently protested "unemployment, exorbitant rents, and tithes" (Dworkin 2012, xxii) and sought to "recover properties seized by settler landlords for non-payment of rent" (Gott 2011, 49). Several lines of evidence converge to validate this view, and so frame Crofton Croker's seemingly anodyne story in a very different light.

The most obvious piece of evidence is the name 'Teigue.' The resonance here is with the names 'Teague' or 'Tadgh,' which served as generic (and abusive) epithets for Irish Catholics in the eighteenth century. (Note the survival of the sectarian term 'Taig' as slang for a Catholic in contemporary Northern Ireland.) Crofton Croker cannot have been unaware of this, but, if corroborative evidence is needed, it can be found in the explanatory note appended to the story. Waxing ethnographic, Crofton Croker dilates on other stories of Teigue, one of which involves him singing a line from a (then) well-known song, "My name is Teigue and I lives in state" (sic). The song in question—"Teague" (Anon., 1841)—is significant: it satirises the Catholic farmer as a well-fed malcontent whose political ambitions are stirred by personal vanity and carousing with the clergy. Crofton Croker is surely trailing his coat here; right down to the creative misspelling that conflates 'Teigue' with 'Teague,' inviting the reader to identify Teigue's wiles with politically aspirant Catholicism.

A second item of evidence comes from the one instance in which Teigue is accorded an anthropomorphic representation. Though several abortive schemes for trapping Teigue are described, the only concrete identification comes when Mr Pratt says that he once fancied he "saw a man in a white frieze jacket pass into the door from the garden to the lawn" (1828, 274). Seemingly incidental, the detail of the "white frieze jacket" would have been a sartorial dog-whistle for an Ascendancy audience. The hardwearing nature of frieze meant that it was the textile of choice for manual labourers—particularly in Ireland, the main export market for English frieze in the nineteenth century. Indeed, the association between frieze and the Irish labourer was such that Samuel Jubb, in his 1860 history of the frieze trade, directs his reader to "the back of an Irish pig-jobber, or that of an Irish reaper" (1860, 45), should he wish to see an instance of worn-out frieze. The qualification of the frieze as "white"— an implausible colour choice for a work garment—functions clearly enough as a reference to the Whiteboys, who were known as such "for the colour of their shirts worn on midnight expeditions" (Christianson 1972, 369).

This linking of Teigue with the Whiteboys is further corroborated by the Whiteboys' own propaganda. They announced themselves as subjects of the mythical 'Queen Sive' and consciously identified with the *aos sí* of popular tradition (Gott 2011, 49). Indeed, one contemporary County Tipperary observer dryly noted, "the fairies are composed of all the able young fellows from Clonmel to Mitchelstown" (Lecky 1891, 355). In this regard, the characteristic Whiteboy activities of levelling ditches, maiming livestock and lighting fires are reminiscent of the mischief popularly attributed to the aforementioned *fir dearg*. If so, Teigue's trickster nature becomes reflective of the Whiteboys' preferred methods of chafing the land-owning classes, through nuisance, aggravation and low-level intimidation.

Viewing the issue more generally, the overall dynamics of the Teigue narrative show yet more convincing parallels with the Whiteboys. Just as domestic servants were omnipresent witnesses to the infractions of the Victorian bourgeoisie (McCuskey 2000), the numerically predominant Catholic agrarian labourers exercised a type of *de facto* moral vigilance with respect to the Ascendency. In this sense, the FSPH offers an intuitively satisfying form for expressing an actual state of affairs—something readily seen in Teigue's familiarity "with every person's acquirements and habits" (1828, 279). Equally, the unpredictable depredations of the Whiteboys can be detected both in Teigue's sporadic comings-and-goings (which may have weeks, months or years between them) and his plural nature (he is reported as being both giant and dwarf). If Teigue is an allegory of a popular movement, his nature clearly cannot coincide with any single agent. Then there is the fact that the Pratt family of the story are *settlers* in Carrigrohane. This can be seen from the fact that Mr Pratt is obliged to describe Teigue and his habits to this brother, Colonel Pratt—something that would be unnecessary were Carrigrohane Manor the ancestral home.

Thus, Teigue directs his actions against the very same class of people singled out by the Whiteboys. (Not that it seems to have hurt them much: the 1876 return of landowners records the extended Pratt family as owning 7,045 acres across County Cork.)

The main evidence *against* the position I am outlining here is the story's puckish tone. If, as I suggest, Crofton Croker's story is a coded record of intra-social antagonism, then one would expect the narrative to exhibit more bite. As it happens, it is delivered in a light-hearted, breezy style that marks it as entertainment rather than allegory. But, this objection fails to take due account of historical context. In the world of "Teigue of the Lee," the genocide of the potato famine has yet to occur, and Anglo-Irish relations have not yet been poisoned by decades of violent sectarianism. It was perfectly possible for an Irish Catholic of the early 1800s to reconcile a desire for regional self-determination and a fairer social dispensation with a warmly held monarchism; indeed, there is evidence that at least some of the Whiteboys did exactly this (Morley 2002). Moreover, even if "Teigue" did suffer from Crofton Croker's tampering hand, it remains broadly consistent with other narratives from popular tradition recorded in the same period. As noted by Mary Helen Thuente, these often exhibit "a passivity, a fatalism, and a reliance on a supernatural dimension" (1985, 133) that is entirely at odds with the project of armed insurrection. At the same time, Thuente identifies a persistently ludic dimension in the representation of agrarian secret societies, citing (for instance) Sir William Wilde's account of a Whiteboy meeting as characterised by a spirit of "frolic—of rude enterprise and adventure in meeting" (1985, 141). Though events like the hanging of thirty Whiteboys in the first four months of 1776 may have cramped the high jinks somewhat, it is probably true that the Whiteboys—like every association of young men from the Indo-European *männerbund* to North American collegiate fraternities—were characterised by initiations, hazings and the jocular exchange of insults. For these reasons, the tone of "Teigue of the Lee," far from telling against its interpretation as a record of social tensions, actually speaks directly to "the portrayal of the outlaw as quick-witted, chivalrous and loath to take human life" (Cashman 2000, 211) typical of the folklore of the period.

In sum, then, a plausible case can be made for the claim that Crofton Croker's "Teigue of Lee" refracts an inherited intuition—the FSPH—through the prism of social relations in late eighteenth- and early nineteenth- century Ireland. The value of using the FSPH in this way is that it gives us occasion to look deeper into a seemingly unremarkable narrative, and detect patterns in it that might otherwise be invisible.

Conversely, investigating empirical results about the mind by way of regional and historical knowledge delivers a more nuanced appreciation of the human cognitive endowment than can ever be achieved in a laboratory setting. To the extent that this is so, "Teigue of the Lee"—its seeming triviality notwithstanding—is expressive of historical and psychological realities that go much deeper than the story's surface concerns.

CONCLUSION

The foregoing material shows the Curse of Macha *rémscel* and "Teigue of the Lee" to have a similar structure, where exploitative social relations are restituted through supernatural action. I maintain that this similarity is not accidental, but is the product of a cross-cultural cognitive disposition that links supernatural agency to moral infractions. As the specific arguments I have made stand or fall by their merits, it is perhaps worth closing with a general comment on the value of cognitive historicism for the study of cultural transmission.

In this regard, I wish to suggest that the cognitive approach offers a vitally important supplement to the genealogical models commonly practised in the analysis of myth and folklore. Typically, these models work on the assumption than the comparative assessment of cultural materials allow for the reconstruction of a (lost) common source, where such a source can be posited to have existed (Puhvel 1989). Implementations of the technique can be found in the work of Georges Dumézil and his school on Indo-European religion (Dumézil 1973; Dumézil 2008; Lyle 2007); more recently, computational models based on phylogenetics have come into vogue (Tehrani 2013; Graça, Tehrani, and Graça 2016; Ross, Greenhill, and Atkinson 2013). Though the results achieved are often worthwhile, there remains an untested assumption that historical factors are sufficient to account for similarities in content or structure. This assumption is likely to be false for two reasons. On the one hand, linguistic parallels suggest that semantic and morphological changes can occur rapidly and irreversibly, often with the effect of making it extremely difficult, if not impossible, to disentangle historical inheritance from local variation (Mallory and Adams 2006, 39–50). On the other, Claude Lévi-Strauss's survey of mythological elaboration in the Americas in his *Mythologiques* (1964-71) argues against the preservation of fixed cultural patterns, and in favour of the local transformation of these patterns by processes of inversion, analogical displacement and substitution. If correct, these objections suggest that the genealogical method may implicitly advocate a game of Chinese whispers as a reliable way of transmitting cultural representations.

This problem is resolved by the cognitive historical approach. Though historical factors always trump cognitive ones in the short term, psychological factors exercise a strongly selective effect in long term transmission chains (Boyer 1999; Morin 2012; Sperber 2006). That is, representations that conform to psychological intuitions and biases are more likely to be both remembered and communicated over the *longue durée* (Braudel 1958). The result is that it becomes possible to say why widely separated texts should exhibit comparable structure, without needing to identify implausible historical connections between them. Moreover, even in cases where there could be a continuity of tradition—as is the case with the two texts discussed here—the cognitive approach explains why some aspects of the tradition are preserved and others are not.

I stress, again, that there is more at work in this process of transmission than merely cognitive constraints; it would be disingenuous to suggest otherwise. Nevertheless, where history is subject to infinite variation, human psychology is not. I would be no less invidious to dismiss the one constant present in every cultural representation. Given this, it seems valid to maintain that historicist and cognitivist approaches are best approached as natural partners, rather than opponents, in the analysis of mythic and folkloric representations. Whether this partnership materialises or not is, of course, an entirely different matter; one thing that is certain is that there is no shortage of material that would reward its pursuit.

James Carney is Wellcome Fellow Medical Humanities at Brunel University London, where he is jointly attached to the Department of Arts & Humanities and the Centre for Culture and Evolution. carneyjp@gmail.com

Author's note: The research in this article was supported by a Marie Skłodowska-Curie Fellowship from the European Commission (grant no. 297854) and a Junior Research Fellowship from Linacre College, Oxford. The material on *Táin Bó Cuailgne*, and the wider theoretical approach informing it, was first presented at the 2014 University of Edinburgh Colloquium, 'Thinking About Celtic Mythology in the 21st Century'; the speculations on 'Teigue of the Lee' were developed subsequent to that meeting. The author would like to thank Michael Gantley for useful discussions and commentary on the latter topic.

References

Anonymous. 1841. "Teague". In *The Dublin Comic Songster: Containing a Choice Collection of Irish, English, and Scottish Comic Songs*, 178–179. Dublin: James Duffy.

Atkinson, Quentin D., and Pierrick Bourrat. 2011. "Beliefs about God, the Afterlife and Morality Support the Role of Supernatural Policing in Human Cooperation." *Evolution and Human Behavior* 32: 41-49.

Atran, Scott. 2002. *In Gods We Trust: The Evolutionary Landscape of Religion*. Oxford: Oxford University Press.

Bateson, Melissa, Daniel Nettle, and Gilbert Roberts. 2006. "Cues of Being Watched Enhance Cooperation in a Real-World Setting." *Biology Letters* 2: 412–414.

Baumard, Nicolas, and Coralie Chevallier. 2012. "What Goes Around Comes Around: The Evolutionary Roots of the Belief in Immanent Justice." *Journal of Cognition and Culture* 12: 67–80.

Bendor, Jonathan, and Piotr Swistak. 2001. "The Evolution of Norms." *American Journal of Sociology* 106: 1493–1545.

Bering, Jesse, and Dominic Johnson. 2005. "'O Lord ... You Perceive My Thoughts from Afar': Recursiveness and the Evolution of Supernatural Agency." *Journal of Cognition and Culture* 5: 118–142.

Bering, Jesse, Katrina McLeod, and Todd K. Shackelford. 2005. "Reasoning About Dead Agents Reveals Possible Adaptive Trends." *Human Nature* 16: 360–381.

Bourrat, Pierrick, Quentin D Atkinson, and Robin I.M. Dunbar. 2011. "Supernatural Punishment and Individual Social Compliance across Cultures." *Religion, Brain & Behavior* 1:119–134.

Boyd, Brian. 2009. *On the Origin of Stories: Evolution, Cognition, and Fiction*. Cambridge MA: Harvard University Press.

Boyer, Pascal. 1999. "Cognitive Tracks of Cultural Inheritance: How Evolved Intuitive Ontology Governs Cultural Transmission." *American Anthropologist* 100: 876–889.

——— 2001. *Religion Explained: The Evolutionary Origins of Religious Thought*. New York: Basic Books.

——— 2003. "Religious Thought and Behaviour as by-Products of Brain Function." *Trends in Cognitive Sciences* 7:119–124.

Budelmann, Felix, and Pauline LeVen. 2014. "Timotheus' Poetics of Blending:

A Cognitive Approach to the Language of the New Music." *Classical Philology* 109:191–210.

Carney, James. 2007. "'Gifts of Heaven--Things of Earth': Haunting and Exchange in Conrad's 'Karain: A Memory.'" *L'Epoque Conradienne* 33:1–17.

———— 2008. "The Pangs of the Ulstermen: An Exchangist Perspective." *Journal of Indo-European Studies* 36:52–66.

———— 2014. "Supernatural Intuitions and Classic Detective Fiction: A Cognitivist Appraisal." *Style* 48:203–218.

Carney, James, Robin Dunbar, Tamás Dávid-Barrett, Anna Machin, and Mauro Silva Júnior. 2014. "Social Psychology and the Comic-Book Superhero: A Darwinian Approach." *Philosophy and Literature* 38A:195–215.

Cashman, Ray. 2000. "The Heroic Outlaw in Irish Folklore and Popular Literature." *Folklore* 111:191–215.

Christianson, Gale E. 1972. "Secret Societies and Agrarian Violence in Ireland, 1790-1840." *Agricultural History* 46:369–384.

Cobley, Paul, and Frederik Stjernfelt. 2015. "Scaffolding Development and the Human Condition." *Biosemiotics* 8:291–304.

Croker, Thomas Crofton. 1828. *Fairy Legends and Traditions of the South of Ireland, Volumes 1-3.* London: John Murray.

De Ste Croix, G.E.M. 1981. *The Class Struggle in the Ancient World: From the Archaic Age to the Arab Conquests.* London: Duckworth.

Dooley, Ann. 2006. *Playing the Hero: Reading the Irish Saga Táin Bó Cúailnge.* Toronto: University of Toronto Press.

Dumézil, Georges. 1973. *Gods of the Ancient Northmen.* Translated by Einar Haugan. Berkeley: University of California Press.

————2008. *Mitra-Varuna: An Essay on Two Indo-European Representations of Sovereignty.* Translated by Derek Coltman. New York: Zone Books.

Dworkin, Denis. 2012. *Ireland and Britain, 1798-1922: An Anthology of Sources.* Cambridge: Hackett Publishing.

Farina, Lara. 2012. "Once More with Feeling: Tactility and Cognitive Alterity, Medieval and Modern." *Postmedieval: A Journal of Medieval Cultural Studies* 3:290–301.

Fehr, Ernst, and Urs Fischbacher. 2004. "Third-Party Punishment and Social Norms." *Evolution and Human Behavior* 25:63–87.

Flack, Jessica C., Michelle Girvan, Frans B. M. de Waal, and David C. Krakauer.

2006. "Policing Stabilizes Construction of Social Niches in Primates." *Nature* 439:426–9.

Gott, Richard. 2011. *Britain's Empire: Resistance, Repression and Revolt.* London: Verso Books.

Graça, Sara, Jamshid J. Tehrani, and Sara Graça. 2016. "Comparative Phylogenetic Analyses Uncover the Ancient Roots of Indo-European Folktales." *Royal Society Open Science* 3:1-11.

Harbus, Antonina. 2012. *Cognitive Approches to Old English Poetry.* Cambridge: DS Brewer.

Henrich, Joseph, Richard McElreath, Abigail Barr, Jean Ensminger, Clark Barrett, Alexander Bolyanatz, Juan Camilo Cardenas, et al. 2006. "Costly Punishment across Human Societies." *Science* 312:1767–70.

Johnson, Dominic. 2005. "God's Punishment and Public Goods: A Test of the Supernatural Punishment Hypothesis in 186 World Cultures." *Human Nature* 16:410–446.

——— 2015. *God Is Watching You: How the Fear of God Makes Us Human.* Oxford: Oxford University Press.

Johnson, Dominic, and Oliver Krüger. 2004. "The God of Wrath: Supernatural Punishment and the Evolution of Cooperation." *Political Theology* 2:159–176.

Jones, F.M.A. 2014. Roman Gardens, Imagination, and Cognitive Structure. *Mnemosyne* 67:781–812.

Jubb, Samuel. 1860. *The History of the Shoddy-Trade: Its Rise, Progress, and Present Position.* London: Houlston and Wright.

Lecky, William Edward Hartpole. 1891. *A History of England in the Eighteenth Century, Volume 4.* London: D. Appleton.

Leverage, Paula. 2010. *Reception and Memory. A Cognitive Approach to the Chanson de Geste.* Amsterdam: Rodopi.

Lévi-Strauss, Claude. 1964-71. *Mythologiques, Vols. I-IV.* Paris: Plon.

Littleton, C. Scott. 1970. "Some Indo-European Themes in the 'Iliad'." In *Myth and Law Among the Indo-Europeans,* edited by Jaan Puhvel, 229–246. Berkeley: University of California Press.

Lyle, Emily B. 2007. "Dumézil's Three Functions and Indo-European Cosmic Structure." *History of Religions* 22:25–44.

Mac Cana, Proinsias. 1983. *Celtic Mythology.* Middlesex: Newnes.

MacCarthy, B.G. 1943. "Thomas Crofton Croker 1798-1854." *Studies: An Irish*

Quarterly Review 32:539–556.

Mallory, J.P. 1989. *In Search of the Indo-Europeans*. London: Thames & Hudson.

———— 1997. The War of the Foundation. In *Encyclopedia of Indo-European Culture*, edited by J.P. Mallory and D.Q. Adams, 631. Chicago: Fitzroy Dearborn.

Mallory, J.P., and D.Q. Adams. 2006. *The Oxford Introduction to Proto-Indo-European and the Proto-Indo-European World*. Oxford: Oxford University Press.

McCuskey, Brian W. 2000. "The Kitchen Police: Servant Surveillance and Middle-Class Transgression." *Victorian Literature and Culture* 28:359–375.

Momigliano, Arnaldo. 1987. "Georges Dumézil and the Trifunctional Approach to Roman Civilization." In *Ottavo contributo alla storia degli studi classici e del mondo antico*, 135–159. Rome: Ed. di Storia e Letteratura.

Morin, Oliver. 2012. "When Does Psychology Drive Culture?" In *Creating Consilience: Integrating the Sciences and the Humanities*, edited by Edward Slingerland and Mark Collard, 179–193. Oxford: Oxford University Press.

Morley, Vincent. 2002. "George III, Queen Sadhbh and the Historians." *Eighteenth-Century Ireland* 17:112–120.

Norenzayan, Ara. 2013. *Big Gods: How Religion Transformed Cooperation and Conflict*. Princeton NJ: Princeton University Press.

O'Brien, Steven. 1997. "Eschatology." In *Encyclopedia of Indo-European Culture*, edited by J.P. Mallory and D.Q. Adams, 180–183. London: Fitzroy Dearborn.

Pereira, Vera, Luís Faísca, and Rodrigo de Sá-Saraiva. 2012. "Immortality of the Soul as an Intuitive Idea: Towards a Psychological Explanation of the Origins of Afterlife Beliefs." *Journal of Cognition and Culture* 12:101–127.

Piazza, Jared, Jesse Bering, and Gordon Ingram. 2011. "'Princess Alice Is Watching You': Children's Belief in an Invisible Person Inhibits Cheating." *Journal of Experimental Child Psychology* 109:311–20.

Puhvel, Jaan 1989. *Comparative Mythology*. Baltimore MD: Johns Hopkins University Press.

Raman, Lakshmi, and Gerald A. Winer. 2004. "Evidence of More Immanent Justice Responding in Adults Than Children: A Challenge to Traditional Developmental Theories." *British Journal of Developmental Psychology* 22:255–274.

Ross, Robert M., Simon J. Greenhill, and Quentin D. Atkinson. 2013. "Population

Structure and Cultural Geography of a Folktale in Europe." *Proceedings of the Royal Society B* 280:1-9.

Sjöblom, Tom. 2000. *Early Irish Taboos: A Study in Cognitive History.* Helsinki: University of Helsinki.

Sperber, Dan. 2006. "Why a Deep Understanding of Cultural Evolution Is Incompatible with Shallow Psychology." In *Roots of Human Sociality: Culture, Cognition and Interaction*, edited by N. J. Enfield and Stephen C. Levinson, 431–452. Oxford: Berg Publishers.

Spolsky, Ellen. 2003. "Cognitive Literary Historicism: A Response to Adler and Gross". *Poetics Today* 24:161–183.

Tehrani, Jamie. 2013. "The Phylogeny of Little Red Riding Hood." *PLOS ONE* 8 doi:10.1371/journal.pone.0078871.

Thomas, Mark G., Michael P.H. Stumpf, and Heinrich Härke. 2006. "Evidence for an Apartheid-like Social Structure in Early Anglo-Saxon England." *Proceedings of the Royal Society B* 273:2651–2657.

Thuente, Mary Helen. 1985. "Violence in Pre-Famine Ireland: The Testimony of Irish Folklore and Fiction." *Irish University Review* 15:129–147.

Yeats, W.B. 1891. *Representative Irish Tales.* New York: G.P. Putnam's Sons.

———— 1892. *Irish Fairy Tales.* London: T. Fisher Unwin.

Zunshine, Lisa. 2006. *Why We Read Fiction: Theory of Mind and the Novel.* Columbus: Ohio State University Press.

The Identification of Shamanism in Celtic Literary and Ethnographic Sources

SHARON PAICE MACLEOD

ABSTRACT. *Several scholarly studies allude to the existence of shamanic elements in Celtic literature, folklore and ethnographical materials. This paper contains a select overview of initial data compiled in relation to a research project in process, to ascertain if the well-documented socio-religious matrix connected with shamanism in other cultural contexts may have existed in Celtic cultural contexts as well.*

KEYWORDS: *shamanism, Celtic literature and culture, shamanic training, Celtic cosmology.*

Scholars have used a number of methodologies to interpret Celtic literature and ethnography. These include multi-disciplinary approaches involving linguistics, archaeology, anthropology, sociology, the study of world religions, Indo-European studies, and comparative folklore and mythology. This paper proposes to add another technique to this analytical toolbox, taken from the field of anthropological studies. First it provides an outline of the often-used but rarely well-defined term 'shamanism,' and within that definition examines Classical accounts, native literature and folklore for examples of this phenomenon in Celtic literary and ethnographic sources. It is hoped that this exercise presents an additional method with which to interpret the rich body of Celtic cultural and literary source materials.

A number of Celtic scholars have referred to shamanic themes or elements in Celtic contexts, and studied specific aspects of shamanism.[1] This article seeks to add to this body of work by providing a concise definition of the term 'shamanism' and providing examples from Celtic contexts to illustrate each element within that definition. It is hoped that this exercise is beneficial to the discipline by providing a base-line definition, and casting a wider net into Celtic source materials than is frequently typical. The paper contains a select overview of data compiled in relation to a research project in process: a comprehensive collection and analysis of elements from Celtic historical, literary and ethnographic materials, to ascertain if the well-documented socio-religious matrix connected with shamanism in other cultural contexts may have existed in Celtic cultural contexts as well.

A DISCUSSION OF METHODOLOGY

The socio-religious complex commonly referred to as 'shamanism' has been recorded and interpreted in a variety of ways, and has been subjected to many forms of analysis by those outside the cultures in question, from initial accounts to the present time. Early ethnographic reports often characterized shamans as mentally ill, suffering from delusions or primitive superstitions, or as charlatans preying upon the fears of their equally superstitious communities. In 1964 the renowned scholar of world religions Mircea Eliade published an influential study of shamanism. Since its publication (and especially in the last few decades), a number of criticisms have been levelled at aspects of his approach and his conclusions (the range and validity of these is beyond the scope of this study). We can note, however, that the field has slowly produced more objective and respectful approaches. A recent academic trend or tendency to analyse shamanism through the lens of modern psychology has prevailed in some sectors: an ethnocentric approach as inappropriate and unfortunate as some of the criticisms levelled at Eliade. More recently, a recognition of the value of traditional wisdom in tribal cultures has begun to permeate the field.[2]

The terms 'world shamanism' or 'universal shamanism' have been widely used (and in some cases, strongly criticized) within the field of anthropology. The bases for this debate are not explored in this study; this would entail a lengthy analysis of work beyond the scope and purpose of this paper. However, noting the challenges involved in using any approach is a necessary response to the debate. The vast array of cultural differences must be taken into account, including differences in symbolism and belief, ritual, and other forms of cultural expression. In support of an argument for the world-wide existence of shamanism (in its various cultural permutations) are: similarities in cosmology, the training and initiation of the shaman, the roles and duties of the shaman, the widespread use of music and sound, and the shaman's ability to enter the otherworld and return at will.

Another challenge specific to this study is the wide range of materials that could be explored in an analysis of Celtic belief. These range from Classical accounts and Romano-Celtic inscriptions, to medieval literary texts and early modern ethnographic accounts, all of which exist within specific regional and temporal contexts with their own sets of concerns and limitations. The difficulties in exploring such a wide range of materials cannot be ignored. In a future full-length work, each proposed element of Celtic shamanism will be illustrated by a larger selection of exemplars, as well as a discussion of context and interpretation. This paper presents only examples for each element, drawn primarily from well-known materials, which I believe helps support the proposed existence of shamanism or shamanic elements in Celtic contexts. An argument for the existence of such a socio-religious complex would be more difficult to support if the illustrative materials were few in number and obscure in nature.

DEFINING SHAMANISM

Shamans all over the world (by whatever name they are known in their respective cultures) are specialists in fostering, restoring and maintaining a harmonious relationship between the inhabitants of this world and the otherworld realms. This is accomplished through a variety of methods, including ritual, divination, and healing ceremonies, and by communicating and interacting with the inhabitants of the spirit worlds. This latter method may involve the invocation of the shaman's spirit allies into this world for guidance or assistance, or the shaman's own journey into the spirit worlds. It is the shaman's ability to travel freely into these realms, performing rituals while so engaged or returning with information that will be of use to the patient or the community, which distinguishes the shaman from other magical practitioners.

A number of elements distinguish shamanic traditions from other types of religious practice. One of the most common is a three-fold cosmology consisting of an Upper World, Middle World and Lower World, with a World Tree, Pillar, Mountain or Cord that connects these worlds. The World Tree is used by the shaman to travel between these cosmic realms. This two-way travel between the worlds is key, for, while other types of spiritual practitioners may call upon the god(s) or spirits for help, the shaman is unique in being able to travel back and forth of his or her own volition between the worlds. Indeed, the shaman is considered a specialist in communicating with the realm of the gods or spirits, as well as working with the soul or spirit (the terminology and nuances of these last vary from culture to culture). Shamans are believed to be able to 'see' what others cannot, they have access to sacred knowledge, and are considered guardians of cultural and religious beliefs and traditions. Shamanic candidates typically undergo a lengthy and intensive training period. Their initiation into shamanic power frequently involves a spiritual or symbolic death and rebirth into a radically altered state of being. This may be preceded by a shamanic illness or madness. Other frequently occurring themes found in connection with shamanic practice are the special costumes, fasting or the ritual ingestion of certain food or substances, specialized languages, knowledge of the natural world, shape shifting, and the use of sound in ritual contexts to facilitate the altered state.[3]

A summary of the primary elements of shamanism may assist in understanding this socio-religious complex, helping to determine if a subject of inquiry falls into the category of shamanism. While many of these elements may be recognizable in other religious or cultural settings, it is their full presence as a 'package'–a cohesive socio-religious phenomenon–that marks the phenomenon of shamanism. The elements associated with shamanism include:

1   cosmology - Three Worlds (Upper, Middle and Lower), often connected by central axis (World Tree, Pillar or Mountain)
2   training – lengthy and intensive, provided by elder shamans and spirits
3   initiation may be preceded by a physical or spiritual illness or madness
4   initiation constitutes a spiritual or symbolic death and rebirth
5   specialist in communicating with the spirit world
6   able to 'see' what others cannot
7   specialist in matters pertaining to the soul or spirit
8   the shamanic journey – two-way travel between cosmic realms
9   shaman performs rituals, healing ceremonies, and divination on behalf of the community
10 widespread use of music and sound to facilitate an altered state of consciousness
11 use of costumes, often with bird or animal symbolism
12 fasting or ritual ingestion of special foods or substances
13 use of specialized shamanic languages
14 access to sacred or otherworldly knowledge or power
15 symbolism associated with shape-shifting
16 guardian of traditional cultural and religious knowledge
17 s/he has knowledge of the natural world in both a physical and symbolic sense

A WORKING DEFINITION

To summarise, the shaman is a religious specialist who performs rituals, healing ceremonies, and divination on behalf of a community. S/he undergoes a lengthy and intensive training at the hands of elder shamans and spirit guides, which may be preceded by a period of illness or madness. Shamanic initiation constitutes a radical transformation – a spiritual or symbolic death and rebirth – into a state of power and specialized ability. The shaman specializes in matters pertaining to the soul, and communicates with the spirit world. Shamans invoke gods and spirits to assist in their work, and undertake journeys to the otherworld realms. This two-way travel, undertaken in relation to a three-fold cosmos, marks out the shaman as different from other religious specialists. Shamanism often involves the use of symbolic costumes, specialized languages, and a variety of common methods to achieve an altered state of awareness. These include music and sound, sensory deprivation or stimulation, and the ingestion of entheogens. The shaman is respected in his or her community as a guardian of cultural and religious knowledge. Shamans are frequently credited with the ability to shape-shift and prophesise; their primary function is to restore and maintain balance between the physical world and the otherworld realms. A lack of balance or reciprocity between the worlds is believed to cause disease and misfortune.[4]

EVIDENCE FOR COSMOLOGY

Many excellent studies of Celtic cosmology provide evidence that the Celts (in various regions and time periods) perceived of a three-fold cosmology. The early Irish perception of a three-fold division of the cosmos into *nem* ('sky'), *muir* ('sea') and *talam* ('earth') is referred to in numerous texts.[5] In addition, early Irish literature contains a number of descriptions of otherworld realms believed to exist under the earth or beneath the waters.[6]

Inscriptions on altars from the Romano-Celtic period refer to deities who may have been associated with the sky realms or Upper World. These include: *Taranis* ('The Thunderer'), *Loucetius* ('Lightning'), *Nodons* ('Cloud-maker') and *Sirona* ('Divine Star Goddess') (Ross 1996, 228-233, 246, 249, 252, 260; Green 1996, 102-104, 135). Deities associated with the Underworld realms are also evident in the archaeological record. In a Gaulish ritual inscription from Chamalières, the god *Maponus* is invoked in his chthonic form. A Gaulish magical tablet from Larzac also appears to refer to a group of women practising a form of chthonic magic (Eska 2002; Koch and Carey 1995, 2-3).

Evidence for the importance of the sacred centre – the location of the

World Tree or Pillar - exists in a number of Celtic literary and archaeological sources (a topic documented by Mac Cana 2011, 73-160). Archaeological excavations have revealed offering pits or shafts located at the center of Celtic religious sites (Raftery 1994, 64-83; Powell 1980, 171-175). Stone pillars were also prominently situated in the centre of Continental Celtic shrines and sanctuaries (Raftery 1994, 180-182; Powell 1980, 162-165). Classical sources refer to an ancient site in Scotland known as *Medionemeton* ('The Sacred Central Place'), which is believed to have been perceived as the cosmological centre of the land (Solway 1981, 673, 713; Rankin 1996, 281). In later times, the sacred centre of Scotland was described by poets as *Taigh nan Teud* ('The House of the String / Cord'), situated near the yew tree of Fortingall, the oldest living tree in Europe and likely associated with a sacred site in ancient times (Newton 2000, 211). In his *De bello gallico* (VI, 13), Caesar mentions that the druids of Gaul gathered at a fixed time each year at a consecrated location in the territory of the Carnutes, which was considered to be the centre of Gaul (Holmes 1914; Ireland 1996, 177). In Ireland, the cosmological centre of the land was the Hill of *Uisneach*, described in one Irish text as the 'navel' of Ireland (Schott 2011, 87-113; Rees and Rees 1995, 159).

A possible related concept is the *bile*, an Old Irish word meaning 'tree or mast,' used especially to refer to ancient and venerated trees. Sacred assemblies were held beneath these trees and it was forbidden to damage them in any way (Mac Cana 2011, 76-79; Ross 1996, 61-62; Rees and Rees 1996, 120). Sacred sites throughout the Celtic world were referred to as a *nemeton*, 'Sacred Place' or 'Sacred Grove' (Mac Cana 2011, 254-259; Rankin 1996, 281). There may be a connection between these arboreal sites and the concept of the World Tree. A passage from an eighth-century Irish text, "Finn and the Man in the Tree," may preserve a symbolic description of the world tree. In the tale, Finn mac Cumhall encounters a man sitting in the top of a tree. There was a blackbird on his right shoulder, a vessel of white bronze containing a trout in his left hand, and a stag standing at the foot of the tree. The man shared hazelnuts, an apple and water from the vessel with the animals (Meyer 1904, 344-349). It is possible that these animals symbolically allude to the three-fold cosmos found in shamanic contexts; the blackbird may symbolize the Upper World, the stag the Middle World, and the trout the Lower World. In support of this assertion are similarities between this passage and descriptions of the Norse World tree, *Ygdrassil*, which involved a similar arrangement of creatures: an eagle and a hawk rested in the upper branches of the tree, harts and goats leapt at its sides, and a serpent lay at its root

(Ellis Davidson 1988, 26-27).

DRUIDIC PARALLELS

It is possible that in the pre-Christian era, the Celtic equivalent of the shamanic specialist may have been the druid. Some Classical authors who wrote about the Celts refer to the high status and respect accorded to the druids, describing them as religious specialists who performed ceremonies, divination and prophecy (Ireland 1996, 176-186). In the mid-first century BCE, Caesar (*De bello gallico*, VI, 13-14) writes that the druids officiated at religious ceremonies, supervised public and private sacrifices, and expounded upon religious questions. In addition, they engaged in discussion about the size and shape of the earth and the universe, and the strength and power of the gods (Holmes 1914; McDevitte 1869; Rankin 1992, 176-179). In the late first century BCE, Diodorus Siculus (V, 31, 2-5) wrote that in Gaul offerings were only made to the gods by the druids, who were considered experts in the nature of the divine and considered to be in communion with it. He described them as philosophers, soothsayers and theologians (Rankin 1996, 272, 274; Ireland 1996, 180-181; Oldfather 1933). In the fourth century, Ammianus Marcellinus described the druids as 'an intimate fellowship of greater ability' who 'rose above the rest by seeking the unseen' (Rolfe 1939; Koch and Carey 1995, 25). Indeed, the word 'druid' (Old Irish *drui* / Middle Welsh *derwydd*) comes from two Indo-European root words, **deru-* ('firm, solid, steadfast') and **wid-* ('to see') (Watkins 2000, 96-97).

Caesar (*De bello gallico*, VI, 14) writes also that those suffering from serious illnesses employed druids to undertake sacrifices on their behalf (Holmes 1914; Ireland 1996, 178). In the first century, Pliny (*Naturalis historia*, XVI, 249-251) describes how the druids ritually gathered mistletoe and undertook a related sacrifice and banquet. The plant was said to have been referred to as 'all-heal' in the Gaulish language, and was believed to impart fertility and serve as an antidote to all poisons (Rackham 1938; Ireland 1996, 183-184). Later in the account (*Naturalis historia*, XXIV, 103-104), Pliny writes about the ritual gathering of a plant referred to as *Selago* (used for eye ailments and to ward off harm) and another called *Samolus* (used to treat pigs and cattle) (Rackham 1938; Ireland 1996, 185).

Like their shamanic counterparts, the druids were particularly concerned with matters pertaining to the soul, and Classical authors repeatedly commented on the druidic preoccupation with the soul. In his *De bello gallico* (VI, 14), Caesar comments that a belief the druids particularly wished to inculcate was that the soul did not perish, but after death passed from one person to another (Holmes 1914; McDevitte 1869; Ireland 1996, 178). Writing at the turn of the first century BCE, Strabo (IV, 4, 4-5) wrote that "the druids and others say that the soul, like the universe, is immortal, though at some time or another both fire and water will overwhelm them" (Ireland 1996, 179). In the first century, Pomponius Mela (*De Chorographia* III, 2, 18-19) said that the druids taught that the soul was eternal and that there was an afterlife (Ireland 1996, 181).

Classical accounts also refer to the training of initiates by the druids. In the pre- and early-Empire period, when the druidic schools were operating in an open and formally organized manner, Caesar made note of a number of pertinent details. In his *De bello gallico* (VI, 13) he says that the druids were held in great esteem, and that large numbers of young men flocked to them for instruction. Some came of their own volition, others were sent by parents or relatives. They reportedly learned a large number of verses by heart, and could remain under instruction for up to twenty years (Holmes 1914; McDevitte 1869; Ireland 1996, 177-178). The Gaulish town of Bibracte, the chief town of the Aedui (near Mount Beuvray, Nièvre) was still a notable druidic school in the early Romano-Celtic period. However, in 12 BCE it was replaced with the Roman town of Augustodunum. Tacitus (*Annales,* 3.43*)* writes that, when the Aedui and Treveri rebelled against the Romans, their goal was to take over Augustodunum, so they could gain control of the young people being educated there (Church and Brodribb 1861; Rankin 1996, 290; Ireland 1996, 185-186).

Pliny (*Naturalis historia* XXX, 13) wrote that, after the revolt of Sacrovir in 21, Tiberius oppressed the learned classes of Gaul (Rackham 1938). However, the druids continued to train their initiates in secret locations, like the later hedge schoolmasters of Ireland. Pomponius Mela (*De Chorographia* III, 2, 18-19) refers to the training of druidic candidates in secret locations - 'hidden glades or caves' (Rankin 1996, 290). Suetonius (*Claudius* 25, 5) reports that, while Augustus had merely forbidden druids to become Roman citizens, in 54, Claudius abolished the whole order. However, Tacitus (*Historiae* IV, 54) describes the druids urging their countrymen to revolt by their chanting (*canebant*) in the period after the death of Vitellius in 69. He also notes the presence of druids in 71 during the revolt of Civilis, prophesying the destruction of Roman power portended by a fire which broke out in the Capitol (Church and Brodribb 1891; Rankin 1996, 290). Over time, the prestige (at least) of druidic training continued, for as late as the fourth century, professors and rhetoricians in Roman Gaul were known to have come from druidic families (Rankin 1996, 233, 243). Like the shamanic initiate, druidic candidates engaged in lengthy and arduous training. Again, Pomponius Mela (*De Chorographia* III, 2, 18-19) writes that druidic training could last up to twenty years. Of course, training may not have always lasted this long, and this detail could reflect either historical reality or Classical perceptions concerning the expertise attributed to the druidic class. It should be noted that the length of shamanic training varies considerably between cultures. In any case, after completing training, the druidic initiate undergoes a radical change of state in terms of ability, authority and social status. While we have no information about the stages of druidic initiation, after the completion of training, the elevated or initiated druidic candidates were apparently able to supervise religious ceremonies, perform divination and healing, and communicate with the divine. They were also qualified to pass down binding legal decisions, intervene between opposing armies, provide advice to their community, and train initiates. Their status was marked by the fact that they were exempt from taxation and military service, as noted by Caesar (*De bello gallico* VI, 14: Holmes 1914; Ireland 1996, 177).

TRAINING IN THE MEDIEVAL PERIOD

Although druids are still mentioned as having some legal status in early Irish law tracts in the ninth century, at some point after the introduction of Christianity, those previously involved in the druidic order either disappeared, or they may have become members of the Christian clergy or a type of learned poet known as a *fili* (plural *filid*) (Kelly 1998, 44, 59-61; Rankin 1996, 243). In the seventh and eighth centuries, when the Irish law tracts were first written down, both druids and *filid* exist in Ireland and have a well-defined legal status in Irish society. It is evident by this point that the *filid* had acquired some of the functions of the druids, as well as some of their social standing (Kelly 1998, 43-49; Caerwyn Williams and Ford 1992, 22-23; Ó Cathasaigh 2014, 121-130).[7] Irish literary sources (like Classical accounts) depict druids in association with rituals, divination, healing, magic, counsel, wisdom, judgements and training students.[8]

Like the druid, the *fili* underwent formal and lengthy training, and their profession was often hereditary. Like their predecessors, they were associated with divination and believed to possess quasi-magical abilities (including satire). They are described as using obscure language or speech, and were sometimes trained in the law. The *filid* were trained to recite a large number of tales and poems, and thus preserved a considerable amount of important cultural information, including history, genealogy, philosophy, and aspects of native belief. In addition to composing complex poetical compositions, the *filid* were believed to have the gift of prophecy.[9] The word *fili* itself comes from an Indo-European root word **wel-* meaning 'to see' (Watkins 2000, 97).

The Irish poetic schools were described in some detail in *The Memoirs of the Right Honourable The Marquis of Clanricarde*, published in London in 1722 and in Dublin in 1744. According to this account, poetic students were expected to gain a thorough knowledge of the history and land of Ireland, compose in complex meters on traditional topics, and master and utilize an archaic form of poetic language. Only those who were descended from poets, had a good memory, and were 'reputed within their tribe,' were candidates for this training. The rooms inside a poetic school were quite plain, but were noted for a remarkable feature: there were no windows to let in the day, nor was any light used at all but that of candles ('and these were brought in at the proper season only'). The school term took place during the darkest time of the year, from November 1st to March 25th. Students were assigned a subject by their teacher at night, and they worked on their composition alone on their beds all the next day, completely in the dark. The following evening, lights were brought in and the students' poems were written down and recited for their instructors (Bergin 1984, 5-8; Caerwyn Williams and Ford 1992, 159-162).

In many cultures, shamanic rituals and ceremonies are performed in darkened spaces or at night. The practice of poets traditionally composing in the dark is mentioned in a number of Irish sources, including a *Dindshenchas* poem on *Bend Etair*: *Cid dorcha dam in lepaid...* ("Thought it be dark to me in my bed...") (Gwynn 1991, III, 110-111). The practice of working and composing in the dark was reported to have been traditional with many known poetic masters, who did not compose in broad daylight (Bergin 1984, 5-8; Caerwyn Williams and Ford 1992, 159-162).

Martin Martin provided a description of poetic schools still active in early eighteenth-century Scotland. Like the Irish students, Scottish poetic candidates used an archaic type of language, and their compositions were performed for their teachers after emerging from their darkened cells. The young poets were said to shut their doors and windows for an entire day, while lying on their beds to compose with a plaid wrapped around their head (Withers and Munro 1999, 79; Bergin 1984, 8-9; Caerwyn Williams and Ford 1992, 162-163). The students placed a stone upon their belly, which may have served to help regulate the breath during the inspirational phase of poetic composition. The Old Irish term *aí*, and the cognate Welsh term *awen* (both deriving from an older form **aui*), denote a type of wisdom or inspiration sought by poets and linguistically associated with the related concepts of breath and inspiration (Watkins 1995, 117; Jarman and Hughes 1992, 16; Ford 1999, xxvii).

The recitation of poetry was governed in some cases by the number of inhalations to be taken during a performance, according to a person's status (Stacey 2007, 76-77, 104, 274n148). The poetic tract *Auraiceipt na n-Éces* states that dithyramb or metrical rhythm (without couplet rhyme or caesura rhyme) was measured by "a word completing a breath which was indicated by the fifth word, for five words are adjudged to be a breath of the poet" (Calder 1995, 70-71). The importance of the breath in poetic contexts is mentioned in several texts.[10] There are also literary references to the use of a magical technique called the 'druidic breath' (Ó Duinn 1992, 37, 75, 79, 91, 99-100).

SUFFERING AND TRANSFORMATION

I now explore Celtic sources for examples of other known elements of shamanism. Magical transformations and rebirth, apparently connected with shape-shifting and the transmigration of the soul, are evident in a number of texts. A well-known example occurs in *Tochmarc Étaine* ('The Wooing of Étain'), where the heroine undergoes a number of transfigurations as a woman, a pool of water and a scarlet fly. In this later form she is swallowed by a warrior's wife and reborn as the woman's daughter (although she does not remember her past life in this incarnation) (Best and Bergin 1992, 323-332; Gantz 1985, 39-59). While this story does not present Étain herself as a shamanic figure, it does provide a clear representation of the theme of shape shifting, a theme which occurs in myths and tales in non-shamanic contexts as well, in connection with belief in the transmigration of the soul.

Other examples of death-and-rebirth exist in the literary sources. Some record illness, madness or suffering prior to a new incarnation. In the medieval Welsh tale *Math Son of Mathonwy,* the young hero Lleu is struck with a poisoned spear under unusual liminal circumstances. He utters a scream and flies off in the shape of an eagle. Later he is found sitting in the top of a tree by his uncle, the magician Gwydion. He sees the eagle's flesh 'rotting away,' signifying his near-death condition. Gwydion sings three magical poems or *englynion*, and, as he does so, the eagle begins to come down from the tree. Gwydion transforms Lleu back into human form, although he is still in a wretched condition. Later Lleu is made whole by a team of healers, and eventually regains authority and power over his rightful kingdom (Williams 1951; Ford 1999b; Davies 2007, 47-64; Ford 1977, 103-107).

In some cultures, members of the community other than the shaman may experience a shamanic illness or ordeal, or acquire some visionary ability (Eliade 2004, 33-66; Halifax 1979, 63-91; Kalweit 1988, 75-93; Eliade 1995.). In some Celtic sources, kings, heroes or commoners are described as having interactions with the otherworld. The greatest of Irish heroes experiences a spiritual illness, as described in *Serglige Con Chulainn* ('The Wasting Sickness of Cú Chulainn'). In the story, Cú becomes perplexed after missing a cast with his spear. He sits with his back against a stone pillar, "for his spirit was angry within him." He falls asleep and sees two women, one clad in a green mantle and one in a purple mantle, who lash him with horsewhips until he is "all but dead." When the Ulstermen perceive his condition, they suggest that he be awakened, but his friend Fergus says, "You shall not move him, for he is seeing a vision." Cú eventually regains consciousness but is ill for an entire year. He recalls having his vision the previous Samhain, and Conchobar advises him to return to the pillar. He does so, and the woman in the green mantle appears before him. She asks for his assistance in the otherworld, and he complies.

While in the otherworld, Cú falls in love with an otherworld woman named Fand. Later, he is confronted by his mortal wife *Emer*, and Fand returns to her supernatural husband. Upon hearing this, Cú makes three great leaps and arrives at Tara Luachra. There he lives in the mountains for a long period of time without food or drink. Emer seeks the assistance of Conchobar, who sends his druids, learned men and people of skill to capture Cú Chulainn. Cú tries to kill them, but, through druidic spells, they are able to bind him and bring him back into society (Dillon 1975, 1-29; Cross and Slover 1996, 176-198). In this tale, a member of society other than the shaman/druid experiences a spiritual illness and travels to the otherworld. Note it is only through the skill of the druids that Cú Chulainn is bound and healed, and restored to his place in the social order.

Other examples of divine madness appear in medieval Irish and Welsh narrative sources. In these tales, men and women known as *geilt* (OIr) or *gwyllt* (MidW) live in a state of near-madness away from society, in the far reaches of the natural world. The Old Irish word *geilt* refers to either a person who goes mad from terror, a panic-stricken fugitive from battle, or an insane person living in the woods, sometimes credited with the power of levitation (Ó Riain 1972; Partridge 1980; Sailer 1997; Bergholm 2012).

One of these figures was Suibhne Geilt, a prince of Ulster who went mad during a battle in 637 and went to live alone in the wilderness. A number of poems are attributed to Suibhne in which he describes his lonely and wretched condition and speaks directly to the inhabitants of the natural world. He wanders restlessly from place to place, "without sense or reason," shunning people, running wildly to the mountains, racing red deer over the moors and sleeping in the woods at night "with no feathers" (O'Keefe 1931; O'Keefe 1913; Murphy 2007, 113-141; Nagy 1982, 44-60). Later in the poem, Suibhne says he has endured many hardships "since feathers grew on my body," possibly a metaphor for a change of physical, spiritual or emotional state.

In similar fashion, the Welsh figure Myrddin goes mad during the Battle of Arfderydd in 573 CE and flees human society to live in the wilderness. Some of his poems are addressed to trees and wild creatures. In the *Black Book of Carmarthen*, a poem attributed to Myrddin mentions the extreme discomfort he endured one night when the snow was up to his thigh, having only wolves for company. In the *Red Book of Hergest*, Myrddin is described as a wise man and a prophet.[11]

Another *geilt*-figure from Irish tradition was the woman Mis, who went mad after seeking the slain body of her father on the battlefield and drinking the blood from his wounds. She fled to the mountains (Sliabh Mis) where she stayed for many years, catching and eating the flesh of anything she encountered, animal or human. Like Sweeney, she could run or fly like the wind. Mis is described as growing something called *clúmh* all over her body, a word which can denote 'feathers' or 'fur'. She was extremely dangerous and many perished attempting to capture her. She was eventually enticed into an interaction with the king's harper, Dubh Ruis, and, as they conversed and interacted, she began to regain her memory. He encouraged her to cook her food rather than eating it raw, and he was eventually able to bathe her. The two slept together, and the act of sexual union improved her condition. Eventually Mis regained her senses, and the fur or feathers that had covered her body disappeared. She married Dubh Rois and returned to society (Ó Cuív 1954, 325-333).

Although exact parallels between shamanic illnesses and the stories of the *geilt / gwyllt* are uncertain (is the mad person a shaman, or are those who cure them shamans?), there do appear to be some connections.

The phenomenon of the *geilt* or *gwyllt* involves a number of elements also present in accounts of shamanic illness or madness. The wildman or woman experiences a physical, emotional or spiritual illness as the result of a traumatic experience (which may have involved an encounter with the dead or the spirit world). S/he leaves society ('the known') and goes to live in the wilderness ('the unknown'). The *geilt* is restless and can travel great distances. S/he may eat or avoid certain foods. The *geilt* is often naked, clothed in rags, or has fur or feathers on their body. S/he appears to be in deep connection with the natural world. The *geilt* experiences visions or hallucinations, and may be anti-social or violent. S/he is able to run swiftly, leap, fly or levitate, and may perch in trees (an activity credited to Hungarian shamans in ethnographic sources). These same activities are sometimes symbolically enacted in shamanic rituals, where they symbolize a spiritual ascent to the Upper World. In relation to this, it is interesting to note that the Old Irish word *geilt* was glossed with the Latin word *volatilis* ('flying') (Ford 1999, xxiv). In these tales, we can note that, either through the completion of certain tasks, as a result of a healing, or simply by surviving their ordeal, in some cases the *geilt* / *gwyllt* figure is able to return to society, transformed by the experience.

SHAPE-SHIFTING AND INSPIRATION

Shape-shifting is an important feature in both shamanic ethnographic and Celtic literary traditions (and in myths and tales from many cultures). The Irish figure *Fintan mac Bóchra* lived to a great age and attained wisdom after spending time in the form of an eagle, a hawk and a one-eyed salmon. In *Lebor Gábala Érenn,* the figure of *Tuan mac Cairill* lived for many generations through a series of metamorphoses as a stag, a boar and an eagle (Carey 1984a; Carey 1984b; Meyer 1907; Koch and Carey 2001, 235-238). In early Irish and Welsh narratives, druids were credited with the power of transforming people into animals or natural elements, or changing one object into another.[12]

In *Lebor Gabála,* the poet Amairgen chants a magical poem which enables the Gaels to experience a change of state and become inhabitants (rather than invaders) of Ireland, a land which had previously been inhabited by the gods alone (Koch and Carey 1995, 265). The poem invokes the wisdom and power of various creatures and elements of the natural world. Here is an excerpt drawn from readings of the various manuscript sources (translation by the author):

I am a wind in a sea
I am an ocean-wave
I am a sound of a sea
I am a stag of attacks
I am a hawk on a cliff
I am a drop of the sun
I am a fair plant
I am a boar for fury
I am a salmon in a pool
I am a lake in a plain...
I am spear among spoils...

Similar poetic utterances were credited to the legendary Welsh poet Taliesin. While tending the fire beneath an elixir of prophetic wisdom created by the magician Cerridwen, a young lad named Gwion Bach obtains three magical drops which endow him with the powers of prophecy, poetry and shape-shifting, Cerridwen is angered, as the magical drops had been intended for her son. She and Gwion Bach engage in a furious pursuit, changing shapes as they go. After shifting into a variety of forms, Cerridwen (in the form of a hen) eats the boy (as a grain of wheat), later giving birth to him in human form and setting him adrift in a coracle. In *The Tale of Taliesin*, the coracle is discovered by a young man named Elphin. When he sees the child he exclaims, "Behold the radiant forehead!" (*tal iesin*), which becomes the name associated to Gwion Bach's rebirth as a poet-seer (Ford 1992; Ford 1977, 164-181). In a medieval Welsh poem credited to Taliesin (*Cad Goddeu* 'The Battle of the Trees'), the poet enumerates various incarnations he experienced before his rebirth, including an eagle, a harp string, a spark in a fire, raindrops, starlight, and an enchanted sword. Taliesin explains that his rebirth did not result from the union of a mortal mother and father, and that he was created from nine forms of elements, trees and flowers, the essence of soil, and the water of the 'ninth wave,' a magical boundary between this world and the otherworld (Haycock 2007, 174-186).

SHAMANIC TECHNIQUES AND SYMBOLISM

Other elements from the shamanic package are present in Celtic literary and ethnographic sources. While some of these elements may be found individually in non-shamanic contexts, it is the presence of all (or nearly all) of these elements *together* that denotes the presence of shamanism (as explained above). Each element could be illustrated with additional (and often numerous) examples from a variety of Celtic contexts. Here I give a few examples to support each element, drawn primarily (though not exclusively) from well-known literary or ethnographic materials.

COSTUME

In many cultures, shamanic costumes feature animal symbolism, especially birds, deer, snakes, horses and bears (Eliade 2004, 145-167, 176-180; Narby and Huxley 2004, *passim*). Bird symbolism is extremely widespread, and the bird may be the most universal of shamanic creatures. Bird feathers, wings or symbols are often incorporated into shamanic headdresses or capes (Eliade 2004, 156-158). Such a garment is described in *Sanas Chormaic*: the text refers to a cloak called a *tuigen* worn by master poets. It was made from white and multi-coloured birds' skins from the waist down, and from mallards' necks and crests from the waist up (Stokes 1868, 160).

In a Middle Irish tale, a quite remarkable costume was worn by the legendary druid Mug Roith, who was trained in a *síd*-mound by an otherworldly druidess. Although blind, Mug Roith could manifest fire and water, alter the landscape, shape-shift, and perform other magical feats. His 'druidic gear' included a bull-hide from a hornless brown bull and a speckled bird-mask with billowing wings. Wearing these, he was said to be able to ascend into the sky. Mug Roith had numerous students, and on one occasions he was assisted by his supernatural teacher's son, who wore a grey-brown mantle decorated with talons, bones and horns (Ó Duinn 1992, 53, 59, 63, 73, 77, 79, 103).

SECRET LANGUAGES

Another common shamanic theme is the use of secret, archaic or ritual languages taught to initiates by tutors or spirit teachers.[13] In the third century, Diogenes Laertius (*Βίοι καὶ γνῶμαι τῶν ἐν φιλοσοφίᾳ εὐδοκιμησάντων*, Prologue, 6) wrote that the druids expounded their philosophy 'in riddles' (Ireland 1986, 182). Secret or obscure language forms, word games and riddles were still used by poets and grammarians in fourth-century Gaul (Rankin 1996, 241-242). In medieval Ireland, poets were credited with using a special 'learned language' (*bérla fortchide na filed*) allegedly unintelligible to those outside of their profession (Chapman Stacey 2007, 98-101; Carey 1996; Watkins 1970).

Riddles and archaic language appear in divinatory contexts in medieval Wales. *Giraldus Cambrensis* noted a specialized class of seers known as the *awenyddion* were said to be led by 'their innate understanding' when answering queries. Once 'taken over' by spirits, they would 'roar out' the response to a question. The *awenyddion* entered into trance states and received messages through visions that came during sleep. Their responses were apparently difficult to understand, but "sounded marvelous nonetheless". After their oracular duties, they were roused by those around them 'as if from a deep sleep,' and did not return to their senses until they were shaken and restored (Jarman and Hughes 1992, 16; Ford 1999. xxvi).

OTHERWORLD JOURNEYS

The 'shamanic journey' refers to the ability to travel between the worlds in a spiritual or ecstatic capacity.[14] Numerous Celtic narratives describe individuals who have encounters with or travel to the otherworld realms. In many cases, once travellers return they describe the remarkable places they have visited, as in *Serglige Con Chulainn* and *Echtrae Cormaic*. In some cases, druids assist travellers with information or prophetic guidance, or provide healing once the journey is over, as in *Serglige Con Chulainn* and *Math uab Mathonwy*.[15] It stands to reason that druids, described as 'experts in communication with the Divine,' were familiar with the otherworld and its inhabitants. First-hand knowledge of these realms would seem to be a prerequisite for guiding or assisting others with their journeys.

Some of such encounters occur in tales known as *echtrae* ('journey,' 'voyage,' 'expedition in quest of adventure') or *immrama* (from Old Irish *imm-rá*, 'travel about' or 'navigate'), often translated simply as 'journey.' In some cases, an inhabitant of the otherworld (in either human or animal form) appears before the journeyer to guide or entice him/her to the otherworld. In other cases, the traveller sets out of his/her own volition. Spirit beings may provide them with a token or amulet to help them accomplish the otherworld journey; in other instances, a verbal invitation is sufficient. The origins, context and interpretation of the *echtrae* and *imramma* constitute a detailed area of research, for which the reader is directed to Duignan (2011), McCone (2000), Mac Mathúna (1985),

Dumville (1976), Loffler (1983), and Mac Cana (1975). I present these two tale genres as potential fruitful areas of inquiry (see forthcoming study).

As is well-known, interactions and journeys between the worlds play a significant role in Celtic folktales and folklore accounts. There are reports of folk-healers and seers undertaking activities which appear to reflect shamanistic elements. One intriguing example concerns a wise woman from one of the Scottish islands. Working with an assistant, she would go into a divinatory slumber in order to find missing boats: "While she slept, her spirit went out to search for the missing boat. But, if the wind changed while she was asleep, she lost her reason." John MacInnes sees this as "a straightforward description of shamanistic trance and the recovery of hidden knowledge" (MacInnes, in Newton, ed. 2006). As research progresses, folklore archives will no doubt play an important role in the exploration of Celtic shamanism.

There are some comparisons we should note in regards to descriptions of otherworld journeys in Celtic contexts and those described in the ethnographic literature. While we do not have direct representations of druids fighting with spirits causing disease, Caesar (*De bello gallico*, VI, 16) comments that druids undertook ceremonies on behalf of the seriously ill. It is possible that these ceremonies involved ritual interaction with spirits believed to cause disease. As we saw above, druids were credited as healers in the literature (as in the narratives of Cú Chulainn and Fand, and Gwyion and Lleu).

Another point to consider is that, in some cultures, shamans undertake the otherworld journey to engage with natural forces for several reasons; they may seek assistance with hunting or bargain for relief from weather conditions. While we do not have evidence for druids as involved with hunting, Caesar (Section 14) says that druids engaged in much discussion about the stars and their motion, the size of the universe and the earth, and the composition of the earth; from which one might suppose that they mediated with elements of the natural world or the cosmos.

Two important areas in which ethnographic reports and the evidence from Celtic contexts agree pertain to magical battles and divination. In several Celtic narratives, druids or magicians fight with other magical practitioners (including story of Cerridwen and Taliesin). Additionally, Classical accounts and native literature are clear that druids engaged in prophecy or divination on behalf of individuals, communities or tribes.

DIVINATION / VISIONARY STATES

A key element of shamanic practice is the use of altered states of consciousness to obtain information. This could take the form of an oracular vision or manifest in a prophetic utterance.[16] An account dating from the second century BCE, attributed to Nicander of Colophon (s.v. Tertullian *De Anima* 57.10), reports that the Celts spent the night near the tombs of their 'famous men' in the hope of receiving a special oracle in their dreams (Koch and Carey 1995, 9). In *Togail Bruidne Dá Derga*, a ritual known as the *tarbfeis* ('bull-sleep') was undertaken in order to reveal the identity of the next king. A bull was offered and consumed, after which the 'priest' (i.e. druid) slept wrapped in its hide. While the druid slept and dreamed, the identity of the king-elect was made known to him (Best and Bergin 1992, 207-245).

As we saw above, Gerald of Wales noted that the *awenyddion* entered into an altered state to obtain knowledge. He wrote that they were consulted about various 'uncertainties' and that those who listened attentively received answers about the information sought.[17] Medieval Irish poets were expected to master three kinds of divinatory techniques: *imbas forosnai* ('great knowledge of illumination'), *díchetal di chennaib* ('extemporaneous incantation of a spell or recitation of a poem'), and *teinm laedo* ('cracking open' or reciting of poems) (Carey 1997, 41-58).

According to Cormac's Glossary, Irish poets could discover whatever they wished to know through *imbas forosnai*. This power was allegedly obtained by chewing on a piece of animal flesh, uttering an incantation, calling upon the gods, and going into a religious 'sleep' (presumably a trance state, for the text mentions this 'sleep' might be only a few minutes in length) (Stokes 1868, 94). During this ritual the subject was watched so he would not be disturbed, a common feature in shamanic rituals, also described in connection with the *awenyddion* and Cú Chulainn's vision.

Chanting and Song – Many shamanic cultures use special kinds of sound or music to help achieve the altered state and thus facilitate healing ceremonies or divination. The shaman may use an instrument with the capacity for producing a great deal of overtones or undertones (natural components of a musical note that differ in pitch and quality from the fundamental tone). These include the drum, the didgeridoo, and certain wind, brass or stringed instruments. In many instances, the shaman and assistants intones, sings or chants to achieve the altered state.[18]

Perceptions or beliefs concerning the power of sound, including music and the spoken word, are omnipresent in Celtic literary sources.[19] Druidic and poetic chanting, recitation, spells and invocations are mentioned with great frequency in both Irish and Welsh narratives, and there are numerous connections between music (vocal and instrumental) and the Celtic otherworld (Ralls-MacLeod 2000).

Caesar (*De bello gallico* VI, 14) noted that the druids trained their initiates through the use of memory and oral tradition, which would have undoubtedly included the chanting or repetition of sacred texts and lore (Holmes 1914; Ireland 1996, 177). Diodorus Siculus mentions the effectiveness of the chanting of druids intervening between opposing armies (Ireland 1996, 180-181; Oldfather 1933). Celtic perceptions about the power of words and sound are evident in the recorded Gaulish belief that the god Ogmios had more power than Heracles. In the second century, the poet Lucan wrote that he saw an image of Ogmios as an old man carrying a club, trailed by a group of willing followers connected by chains of amber and gold to the deity's tongue; a bystander informed him that the picture meant that the power of the word was more potent than physical strength, and that age and experience contributed to the growth of eloquence (Carey 2014).

In terms of musical instruments, narratives refer to an object known as the *craeb-síde* or *craeb-sidamail* (*síd* or 'fairy' branch). This was apparently a branched wand or staff from which bells were suspended, whose sound had magical and healing properties (Ralls-MacLeod 2000, 62; Hull 1901). It may have had a parallel in bell-branches used to mark the status of poets: a bronze branch for lower orders, a silver branch for the *anruth*, and a golden branch for the *ollam* (Breatnach 1987). Archaeologists have found what seem to be ritual objects of the kind commonly referred to as a 'bull-roarers', from Iron Age Ireland and Scotland; examples are found in the Ulster Museum and the National Museum of Scotland. This simple but effective instrument consists of a long, narrow blade of wood or bone with a hole at one end, through which a piece of string or sinew is attached. The blade is whirled in a circle and produces a remarkably loud whirring sound; similar objects are sometimes used in shamanic and initiation rites.[20]

FASTING, OR ALTERNATELY, THE CONSUMPTION OF SPECIAL SUBSTANCES

In many shamanic contexts, music or sound is the primary or sole method used to induce an altered state of consciousness. Sensory deprivation (fasting, isolation, darkness) can be used to similar effect, as can sensory overstimulation (dancing, clapping, or percussion). Many accounts cite the ingestion of specialized (and frequently entheogenic) foods or substances to cause altered states of awareness.[21]

In one of Pliny's descriptions of the gathering of healing plants by druids (*Naturalis historia* XXIV, 104), he writes that they fasted prior to undertaking this ritual activity (Rackham 1938; Ireland 1996, 185). In medieval Ireland, ritual fasting was a legally recognized method for obtaining justice (Kelly 1998, 182). The MacCrimmons, the hereditary pipers of Clan MacLeod, were reported to fast for two days when faced with a formidable mental or creative task, like the composition of a *pibroch*. They were said to have obtained their gift of music from the otherworld (Newton 1999, 332-334).

Throughout Celtic literature and folklore records, there are notable stories pertaining to the consumption of certain foods or substances (salmon or animal flesh, hazelnuts, red berries or apples) which appear to have facilitated contact or communication with the otherworld and provided access to divine wisdom or inspiration. In *Sanas Chormaic*, a person in search of *imbas* chewed on a piece of animal flesh. Finn mac Cumhaill obtained the gift of prophecy by eating salmon flesh (or later, by chewing on his thumb which had touched the fish). Taliesin acquired his skill by drinking three drops of a potent herbal brew. It is possible that these narratives involve the use of *noa* terms (terms of avoidance) or coded language concerning the ingestion of entheogenic substances, a line of inquiry I am currently investigating.[22]

MAINTAINING A RECIPROCAL RELATIONSHIP WITH THE OTHEWORLD

While the shaman clearly has many roles and functions, the sum total of these and their desired effects can effectively be summed up in a single phrase: maintaining a balanced and reciprocal relationship between the physical and non-physical worlds. Illness and misfortune were believed to be caused by imbalances or intrusions, and the shaman specialized in achieving an altered state of consciousness in order to gain information about or rectify these situations.[23] Perceptions concerning natural balance or imbalance, and the importance of reciprocity, have intriguing parallels in the Celtic source materials.

As is widely known, Celtic narratives from the medieval period and folklore reports from the early modern era exhibit a shared focus on the continuous (and complex) interaction between human beings and inhabitants of the otherworld. In Ireland, the earliest name for the latter was the *Síabhra* or the *Áes Síde* (Carey 1991; Carey 1984). The word *síd* comes from an Indo-European root *sed* meaning 'seat' (as in the 'seat' or 'abode' of the gods). It has a secondary meaning of 'peace' (Sims-Williams 1990, 57-81). The word *síd* seems to have first been used to refer to sacred places: *síd*-mounds or other locations where one might encounter the inhabitants of the otherworld. It was then also used to refer to these beings themselves (as in the term *Áes Síde*). The word may have then acquired a third meaning, 'peace,' not an eternal or guaranteed state, but referring to the peace and prosperity that resulted from the ability to recognise, respect and maintain right relationship with the otherworld (Ó Cathasaigh 1978).

If these correlations are correct, a concern with balance and reciprocity between the worlds formed an important part of Celtic belief structures. Celtic folktales and folklore discuss at length the importance of avoiding, placating or gaining the blessings of the fairy folk. This theme played out in the medieval literature as well, often in more convoluted forms. There are two particularly clear examples of this theme of alliance and reciprocity, one from an Irish context and one from a Welsh narrative, with which I conclude this study.

In the early Irish tale *Echtra Cormaic* ('The Adventures of Cormac'), the god Mannanán mac Lir entices King Cormac to the otherworld and gives him a vision of an otherworld well of wisdom. He then gives Cormac a magic branch and a cup with which to discern between truth and falsehood. When Cormac asks Manannán if they might form an alliance the deity says he is "well pleased" with the idea (Hull 1949; Ó Cathasaigh 1977, 80-85; Cross and Slover 1996, 503). In a medieval Welsh source, the First Branch of the Mabinogi, King Pwyll has inadvertently offended an otherworld king named Arawn. Pwyll asks Arawn how he can "gain peace" with him. After proving himself in the otherworld, the two become allies, thereafter exchanging gifts and respect (Thomson 2002; Davies 2007, 3-21; Ford 1977, 38, 42)

CONCLUSION

It is hoped that this article has served to establish a reasonable argument for the possible existence of shamanic elements (and perhaps a form of European shamanism) among at least some of the Celtic-speaking peoples. This short account shows that evidence for the elements of shamanism may be found throughout the corpus and in almost every time period. This brief overview has primarily made use of well-known sources; indeed, much of this material will be familiar to readers involved in Celtic studies, underscoring the permeation of this socio-religious phenomenon in Celtic cultural contexts. One does not need to dig too far in order to produce a fairly substantial body of evidence for each of the primary and requisite elements of shamanism.

While some scholars have noted specific instances of shamanic elements in Celtic literary and ethnographic sources, this article seeks clearly to define, outline and demonstrate the possible (and even probable) existence of a socio-religious phenomenon that may be referred to as 'Celtic shamanism.' This would constitute a detailed field of study, one that is currently under investigation. This paper is intended as an introduction to this body of research, and seeks to provide a well-defined and user-friendly introduction to this material for Celticists, folklorists and other scholars, initiating a comparative approach to a complex topic that deserves to be more fully explored.

Sharon MacLeod trained in Celtic studies at Harvard University. She is the author of Celtic Myth and Religion, Queen of the Night, *and* The Divine Feminine in Ancient Europe. *She has studied with Gaelic, Lakota and Andean elders and is the Director of Immrama: Indigenous Celtic Shamanic Traditions.*

Notes

1   Chapman Stacey (2007, 86, 151-153); Rankin (1996, 52, 267, 277-278, 280); Caerwyn Williams and Ford (1992, 32); Jarman and Hughes (1992, 15); Watkins (1995, 117-119); Sjoestedt (1982, 113); Rees and Rees (1995, 17, 236, 256, 305, 310); Waddell (2014); Bondarenko (2014); Bergholm (2012); Jones (1998); Nagy (1981); Melia (1983); Ó hOgain (1998); Trevarthan (2003); Lonigan (1985); and studies appearing in Borsje, Dooley, Mac Mathúna and Toner (2014).

2   An exposition of the historiography of shamanism is outlined in Narby and Huxley (2004) and discussed by Rank (1967).

3   It is important to note that shamanism may co-exist with other religious systems, and its techniques and symbolism may survive even when other systems are introduced or predominate. For example, Andean shamanic traditions co-exist with Catholicism, Nepalese shamans who work in the same community with Buddhist practitioners and sometimes incorporate

elements of Buddhism into their practices (and vice versa), and forms of shamanic practice in India which thrive in spite of a Hindu majority (Pentikainen 1997; Pócs 2005; Znamenski 2003; Vitebsky 2001; Narby 2004; Eliade 2004).

4   Rank 1967; Glosecki 1989; Ellis Davidson 1988; Pentikainen 1997; Pócs and Klaniczay 2004; Vitebsky 2001; Eliade 2004; Kalweit 1988; Eliade 1995; Halifax 1979; Narby and Huxley 2004. The interested reader may also consult Miller 2002. Information about the elements of shamanism in this discussion have been derived from ethnographic sources, secondary literature, and fieldwork pertaining to shamanic traditions in North America (Lakota), South America (Q'ero) and Asia (Nepal). I would especially like to thank Wicasa Wakan Tim Swallow (Lakota, Pine Ridge Reservation) and Paqo Don Martin Piñedo (Cusco, Peru), and the shamanic specialists C.A. Roberge and M.R. Verrilli for their generosity in sharing knowledge and experience, and for providing detailed information and culturally appropriate understanding of these traditions.

5   Mac Mathúna 2014, 10-33; Mac Mathúna 1999, 174-187; Mac Mathúna 1997, 532-547; Carey 1991, 154-159; 1982.

6   Mac Mathúna 1999, 174-187; Mac Mathúna 1997, 532-547; Cross and Slover 1996, 188-190, 503-507, 588-595.

7   The druids seem to have had a good reputation in Ireland longer than on the Continent (Kelly 1998, 59-61; Rankin 1996, 292-293).

8   Ó Cathasaigh 2014, 199, 228, 233-234, 238-247, 264-265, 272-273, 403-404; Micheelsun 2007; Piggott 1993, 96-109; O' Rahilly 1976, 132, 142-143, 216-217; Dillon 1975, 9, 29; Dillon 1952, 72n6; Best and Bergin 1992, 244-245; Ní Dhonnchada 1964, lines 734-744; Ó Duinn 1992; Hull 1934; and Williams M. 2010, Chapter Two.

9   Kelly 1998, 43-49; Caerwyn Williams and Ford 1992, 22-44; Chapman Stacy 2007, 82-89, 157-164; Breatnach L. 1987; Breatnach, L. 1984; Breatnach, P. 1983; Caerwyn Williams 1996; Carey 1995; Rowlands 1985; Caerwyn Williams 1971.

10 Calder 1995, lines 930-931, 3528, 3860; and Gwynn 1940, 35-40. A translation of the relevant section of the latter is currently under

preparation by the author.

11 Jarman and Hughes 1992, 102-106; Jarman 1970; Jarman 1967; Jarman 1959; Williams 1954, 32.

12 O' Rahilly 1976,142-143, 216-217; Dillon 1975, 9, 29; Best and Bergin 1992, 244-245; Ó Duinn 1992 passim.

13 Eliade 2004, 62, 93, 96-99, 288, 290, 338, 347, 440, 496, 511; Kalweit 1988, 95, 100, 152; Vitebsky 2001, passim).

14 Kalweit 1988, 31-55; Halifax 1979, 35-62; Eliade 2004, passim; Vitebsky 2001, passim.

15 Dillon 1975, 15-29; Carey 1994; Hull 1949; Ó Cathasaigh 1977, 24, 47, 61, 80; Ford 1999; Davies 2007, 62-64; Cross and Slover 1996, 197-198, 503-507.

16 Eliade 2004, 176, 184, 228, 239, 249, 297, 364, 382, 391, 442; Kalweit 1996, passim; Narby and Huxley 2004, passim; Vitebsky 2001, passim.

17 Caerwyn Williams and Ford 1992, 161-162; Jarman and Hughes 1992, 16; Ford 1999, xxvi.

18 Excellent examples are provided in, Kalweit 1988, 80, 82, 103-104, 116, 121, 144-159, 177, 179, 225-230; and Eliade 2004, 19, 83, 91, 96, 100, 175, 180, 222-223, 290, 303, 335, 358.

19 Carey 2014; McLaughlin 2008; Chapman Stacey 2007; Carey 1997; Watkins 1995; Breatnach 1984; Caerwyn Williams and Ford 1992; Jarman and Hughes 1992.

20 For initiation rituals, see Eliade 1995. For an excellent discussion about the bullroarer and its possible inclusion in a Middle Irish saga pertaining to the druidic figure of Mog Ruith, see Chadbourne 1994.

21 Detailed examples may be found in, Kalweit 1992, 150, 160-174, 195-200, 226-228) and Eliade 2004, 24, 29, 43, 64, 73, 84, 109, 128-131, 168-180, 220, 247, 303-304, 340, 417, 440, 449, 451, 459, 461.

22 Paice MacLeod, 2000; also updated and forthcoming as 'Gods, Poets and Entheogens, Ingesting Wisdom in Early Irish Literary Sources,' in Lyle, Emily, ed., Celtic Myth in the 21st Century: The Gods and their Stories in a Global Perspective, University of Wales Press, 2018.

23 Kalweit 1988, 12, 43-45, 59-70, 229-232; Halifax 1979, 18-22; Eliade 2004, 23, 215-216, 508; Dubois 2009; Vitebsky 2001. I am indebted to Tim Swallow, Don Martin Piñedo, Dr. M.R. Verrilli and Dr. C.A. Roberge for confirmation that this important theme of balance and reciprocity does indeed form part of shamanic practices and continues to be an important factor, if not the most important guiding principle.

References

Bergholm, Alexandra. 2012. *From Shaman to Saint: interpretive strategies in the study of Buile Shuibhne.* Helsinki: Scientiarum Fennica.

Bergin, Osborn. 1984. *Irish Bardic Poetry.* Dublin: Dublin Institute for Advanced Studies.

Best, R.I. and Osborn Bergin. 1992. *Lebor na hUidre – Book of the Dun Cow.* Dublin: Dublin Institute for Advanced Studies.

Bondarenko, Grigory. 2014. *Studies in Irish Mythology.* Berlin: Currach Bhán Publications.

Borsje, Jacqueline, Ann Dooley, Séumas Mac Mathúna and Gregory Toner, Gregory, eds. 2014. *Celtic Cosmology: Perspectives from Ireland and Scotland.* Toronto: PIMS.

Breatnach, Liam. 1987. *Uraicecht na Ríar.* Dublin: Dublin Institute for Advanced Studies.

——— 1984. "Canon Law and Secular Law in early Ireland: the significance of *Bretha Nemed.*" *Peritia* 3:439-459.

Breatnach, Pádraig. 1983. "The Chief's Poet." In *Proceedings of the Royal Irish Academy, vol. 83 C,* 37-79.

Bridgeman, Timothy P. 2005. *"Keltoi, Galatai, Galli:* Were They All One People?" In vol. 25 of *Proceedings of the Harvard Celtic Colloquium,* edited by Christina Chance et al., 155-162. Cambridge and London: Harvard University Press.

Caerwyn Williams, J.E. 1996. "The Celtic Bard." In *A Celtic Florigelium – Studies in Memory of Brendan O hehir,* edited by Kathryn A. Klar, Eve E. Sweetser, and Claire Thomas, 216-226. Lawrence MA: Celtic Studies Publications.

——— 1971. "The Court Poet in Medieval Ireland." In *Proceedings of the British Academy,* vol. 57, 85-135. Oxford: Oxford University Press.

Caerwyn Williams, J.E., and Patrick K. Ford. 1992. *The Irish Literary Tradition.* Cardiff / Belmont: University of Wales Press / Ford and Bailie.

Calder, George. 1995. *Auraceipt na n-Éces.* Dublin: Four Courts Press.

Carey, John 2014. "Ogmios and the Eternal Word." *Cosmos: The Journal of the Traditional Cosmology Society* 30:1-35.

———— 1997. "The Three Things Required of a Poet." *Ériu* 48:41-58.

———— 1996. "Obscure Styles in Medieval Ireland." *Mediavalia: A Journal of Medieval Studies* 19:23-39.

———— 1994. "The Uses of Tradition in *Serglige Con Chulainn.*" In *Ulidia,* edited by J. P. Mallory and G. Stockman, 77-84. Belfast: December Publications.

———— 1991. The Irish 'otherworld': Hiberno-Latin Perspectives." *Éigse* 25:154-159.

———— 1984a. "Scél Tuain meic Chairill." *Ériu* 35:93-111.

———— 1984b. "Suibhne Geilt and Tuán mac Cairill." *Éigse* 20:93-105.

———— 1982. "The Location of the Otherworld in Irish Tradition." *Éigse* 19:36-43.

Chadbourne, Kathryn. 1994. "Giant Women and Flying Machines." In vol. 14 of *Proceedings of the Harvard Celtic Colloquium,* edited by Pamela S. Hopkins and Laurance J. Maney, 106-114. Cambridge and London: Harvard University Press.

Chapman Stacey, Robin. 2007. *Dark Speech – The Performance of Law in Early Ireland.* Philadelphia: University of Pennsylvania Press.

Church, Alfred J. and William J. Brodribb. 1861. *Tacitus – Annals.* Oxford: Oxford University.

Cross, Tom P. and Clark H. Slover. 1996. *Ancient Irish Tales.* New York: Barnes and Noble.

Dillon, Myles. 1975. *Serglige Con Culainn.* Dublin: Dublin Institute for Advanced Studies.

———— 1952. "The Story of the Finding of Cashel." *Ériu* 16:61-73.

Dinneen, Patrick S. 1980. *Forus Feasa ar Éirinn: The History of Ireland by Geoffrey Keating.* London: Irish Texts Society.

Dubois, Thomas A. 2009. *An Introduction to Shamanism.* Cambridge: Cambridge University Press.

Duignan, Leonie. 2011. *The Echtrae as an Early Irish Literary Genre.* Rahden/

Westf.: Verlag Marie Leidorf.

Dumville, David. 1976. "*Echtrae* and *Immram*: Some Problems of Definition." *Ériu* 27:73-94.

Eliade, Mircea. 2004. *Shamanism: Archaic Techniques of Ecstacy.* Princeton: Princeton University Press.

————— 1995. *Rites and Symbols of Initiation.* Woodstock: Spring Publications.

Ellis Davidson, Hilda. 1988. *Myths and Symbols in Pagan Europe: Early Scandinavian and Celtic Religions.* Syracuse: Syracuse University Press.

Eska, Joseph. 2002. "Remarks on Linguistic Structures in a Gaulish Ritual Text." In "Indo-European Perspectives", edited by R.V. South, special issue, *Journal of Indo-European Studies* 43:33-59.

Ford, Patrick K. 1999. *The Celtic Poets.* Belmont: Ford and Bailie.

————— 1999b. *Math uab Mathonwy.* Belmont, MA: Celtic Studies Publications.

————— 1992. *Ystoria Taliesin.* Cardiff: University of Wales Press.

————— 1977. *The Mabinogi and other Medieval Welsh Tales.* Berkeley: University of California Press.

Gantz, Jeffrey. 1985. *Early Irish Myths and Sagas.* Harmondsworth: Dorset Press.

Glosecki, Stephen O. 1989. *Shamanism and Old English Poetry.* New York and London: Garland.

Green, Miranda. 1998. *Animals in Celtic Life and Myth.* London: Routledge.

————— 1996. *Celtic Goddesses.* New York: George Braziller.

Gwynn, Edward J. 1991. *The Metrical Dindshenchas.* Dublin: Dublin Institute for Advanced Studies.

————— 1940. "An Old-Irish Tract on the Privileges and Responsibilities of Poets." *Ériu* 13 (Pt. 1): 1-60.

Halifax, Joan. 1979. *Shamanic Voices – A Survey of Visionary Narratives.* New York: Dutton.

Haycock, Marged. 2007. *Legendary Poems from the Book of Taliesin.* Aberystwyth: Cambrian Medieval Celtic Studies.

Herity, Michael and George Eogan. 1996. *Ireland in Prehistory.* New York: Routledge.

Holmes, T. Rice.1914. *Gaius Julius Caesar – Commentarii de bello Gallico.* Oxford: Clarendon Press.

Hull, Vernam. 1949. *"Echtra Cormaic maic Airt*, 'The Adventures of Cormac mac Art.'" In *Publications of the Modern Language Association of America* 64:871-883.

——— , ed. and trans. 1934. "The Conception of Conchobor." In *Irish Texts*, edited by J. Fraser, P. Grosjean, and J.G. O'Keefe, fasciculus 4, 4-12. London: Irish Texts Society.

Hutchison, David A. 2009. "Links to Pagan Ritual in Medieval Irish Literature." *Études Irlandaises* 34:113-143.

Ireland, Stanley. 1996. *Roman Britain: A Sourcebook*. London: Routledge.

Jarman, A.O.H. 1970. *The Legend of Merlin*. Cardiff: University of Wales Press.

——— 1967. *Ymddiddan Myrddin a Thaliesin*. Caerdydd.

——— 1959. "The Welsh Myrddin Poems." In *Arthurian Literature in the Middle Ages*. Edited by R.S. Loomis, 20-30. Oxford: Oxford University Press.

Jarman, A.O.H. and Gwilym Rees Hughes. 1992. Vol. 1 of *A Guide to Welsh Literature*. Cardiff: University of Wales Press.

Jones, Leslie. 1998. *Druid – Shaman - Priest: Metaphors of Celtic Paganism*. Enfield Lock, Middlesex: Hisarlik.

Kalweit, Holger. 1988. *Dreamtime and Inner Space – The World of the Shaman*. Boston: Shambhala.

Kelly, Fergus. 1998. *A Guide to Early Irish Law*. Dublin: Dublin Institute of Advanced Studies.

Koch, John T. and John Carey, eds. 1995. *The Celtic Heroic Age*. Oakville and Aberystwyth: Celtic Studies Publications.

Loffler, C.M. 1983. *The Voyage to the Otherworld Island in Early Irish Literature*. Salzburg.

Lonigan, Paul. 1985. "Shamanism in the Old Irish Tradition." *Eire* 20 (Pt 3): 109-129.

Mac Cana, Proinsias. 2011. *The Cult of the Sacred Centre: Essays on Celtic Ideology*. Dublin: Dublin Institute for Advanced Studies.

——— 1975. "On the prehistory of *Immram Brain*." *Ériu* 27:33-52.

Mac Mathúna, Liam. 2014. "The Irish Cosmos Revisited: Further Lexical Perspectives." In *Celtic Cosmology: Perspectives from Ireland and Scotland*. Eds. Jacqueline Borsje, Ann Dooley, Séumus Mac Mathúna, and Gregory Toner. Toronto: PIMS.

——— 1999. "Irish Perceptions of the Cosmos." *Celtica* 23:174-187.

———— 1997. "The Christianization of the Early Irish Cosmos? *muir mas, nem nglas, talam cé.*" In *Zeitschrift fur Celtische Philologie 45-50*, 532-547.

Mac Mathúna, S. 1985. *Immram Brain: Bran's Journey to the Land of the Women.* Tubingen.

Matonis, A.T.E. and Daniel Melia, eds. 1990. *Celtic Language, Celtic Culture: A Festschrift for Eric P. Hamp.* Van Nuys: Ford and Bailie.

McCone, Kim. 2000. *Echtrae Chonnlai and the Beginnings of Irish Vernacular Literature.* Maynooth: An Sagart.

————. 1990. *Pagan Past and Christian Present in Early Irish Literature.* Maynooth: An Sagart.

McDevitte, W.A. and W.S. Bohn. 1869. *Julius Caesar – The Gallic Wars.* New York: Harper and Brothers.

McLaughlin, Roisin. 2008. *Early Irish Satire.* Dublin: Dublin Institute for Advanced Studies.

Melia, Dan. 1983. "Law and the Shaman Saint." In *Celtic Folklore and Christianity,* edited by Patrick K. Ford, 113-128. Los Angeles: University of California Press.

Meyer, Kuno. 1907. "Colloquoy between Fintan and the Hawk of Achill." In vol. 1 of *Anecdota from Irish Manuscripts,* edited by O. J. Bergin et al., 24-39. Halle a.S.: M. Niemeyer; Dublin: Hodges, Figgis & Co.

———— 1904. *Finn and the Man in the Tree.* Dublin: R.I.A. Todd Lecture Series.

Micheelsen, Arun. 2007. "King and Druid." In vol. 20/21 of *Proceedings of the Harvard Celtic Colloquium,* edited by Hugh Fogarty et al., 98-111. Cambridge and London: Harvard University Press.

Miller, Anne L. 2002. "Shamanism: A Selected Annotated Bibliography." ANSS: The Anthropology and Sociology Section of the Association of College and Research Libraries (ACRL). http://anssacrl.wordpress.com/publications/bibliographies/annual-program-2002/.

Narby, Jeremy and Frances Huxley. 2004. *Shamans Through Time.* New York: Tarcher.

Nagy, Joseph F. 1982. "The Wisdom of the Geilt." *Éigse* 19:44-60.

———— 1981. "Shamanic Aspects of the *Bruidhean* Tale." *History of Religions* 20:302-322.

Newton, Michael. 2006. *Dùthchas nan Gàidheal – Selected Essays of John MacInnes.* Edinburgh: Birlinn.

———— 2000. *A Handbook of the Scottish Gaelic World.* Dublin: Four Courts Press.

———— 1999. *"Bha mi 's a' chnoc*: Creativity in Scottish Gaelic Tradition." In *Proceedings of the Harvard Celtic Colloquium,* vol. 19, 312-339. Cambridge and London: Harvard University Press.

Ní Dhonnchadha, L. 1964. *"Aided Muirchertaig Meic Erca."* *Medieval and Modern Irish Series,* vol. 19, 1-73. Dublin: Dublin Institute for Advanced Studies.

Ó Cathasaigh, Tomás. 2007. "Early Irish Literature and Law", lecture presented at the Annual Meeting of the Finnish Society of Sciences and Letters, April 27, *2007, now in Sphinx: Yearbook of the Finnish Society of Sciences and Letters,* edited by Peter Holmberg, 111-119.

———— 1996. "Early Irish Narrative Literature." In *Progress in Medieval Irish Studies,* edited by K. McCone and K. Simms, 55-64. Maynooth: An Sagart.

———— 1984. "Pagan Survivals: The Evidence of Early Irish Narrative." In *Ireland and Europe: The Early Church,* edited by. P. Ní Chatháin and M. Richter, 291-307. Stuttgart: Klett-Cotta.

———— 1978. "The Semantics of *Síd." Éigse* 17:137-155.

———— 1977. *The Heroic Biography of Cormac mac Airt.* Dublin: Dublin Institute for Advanced Studies.

Ó Duinn, Sean. 1992. *Forbhais Droma Dámhgháire.* Dublin: Mercier Press.

Ó hOgain, Daithi. 1998. "The Shamanic Image of the Irish Poet." In *That Other World: The Supernatural and the Fantastic in Irish literature and its Contents.* Edited by Bruce Stewart, 12-48. Gerrards Cross: Colin Smythe.

O'Keefe, J.G. 1931. *Buile Shuibhne.* Medieval and Modern Irish Series 1. Dublin: Dublin Institute for Advanced Studies.

———— 1913. *Buile Shuibhne Geilt.* Irish Texts Society 7. London: Irish Texts Society.

Oldfather, C.H. 1933. *Diodorus Siculus* – Loeb Classical Library. Cambridge: Harvard University Press.

O'Rahilly, Cecile. 1976. *Táin Bó Cúailgne – Recension* I. Dublin: Dublin Institute for Advanced Studies.

Ó Riain, Padraig. 1972. "A Study of the Irish Legend of the Wild Man." *Éigse* 14:179-206.

Paice MacLeod, Sharon. 2012. *Celtic Myth and Religion: A Study of Traditional Belief.* Jefferson NC / London: McFarland Publishers.

───── 2018. "Gods, Poets and Entheogens: Ingesting Wisdom in Early Irish Literary Sources," in *Celtic Myth in the 21st Century: The Gods and their Stories in a Global Perspective,* edited by Emily Lyle. Cardiff: University of Wales Press.

───── 2000. *The Hazel of Immortality: Entheogens in Celtic Literary and Ethnographic Contexts.* Honorarium lecture, GSAS / Ford Foundation Lecture Series, Harvard University, December 12th 2000.

Partridge, Angela. 1980. "Wild Men and Wailing Women." *Éigse* 18 (Pt 1): 25-37.

Pentikainen, Juha. 1997. *Shamanism and Culture.* Helsinki: Etnika Co.

Piggott, Stuart. 1993. *The Druids.* New York: Thames and Hudson.

Pócs, Eva and Gabor Klaniczay. 2004. *Communicating with the Spirits.* Budapest / New York: Central European University Press.

Powell, T.G.E. 1980. *The Celts.* London: Thames and Hudson.

Quin, et al. 193-1976. *Dictionary of the Irish Language.* Dublin: Royal Irish Academy.

Rackham, H. 1938. *Pliny – Natural History.* Loeb Classical Library. Cambridge: Harvard University Press.

Raftery, Barry. 1994. *Pagan Celtic Ireland.* London: Thames and Hudson.

Ralls-MacLeod, Karen. 2000. *Music and the Celtic Otherworld.* Edinburgh: Edinburgh University Press.

Rank, Gustav. 1967. "Shamanism as a Research Subject: Some Methodological Viewpoints." In *Studies in Shamanism,* edited by C.M. Edsaman, 15-22. Stockholm: Almqvist.

Rankin, David. 1996. *Celts and the Classical World.* London: Routledge.

Rees, Alwyn and Brinley. 1995. *Celtic Heritage.* New York: Thames and Hudson.

Ritari, Katja and Alexandra Bergholm, eds. 2008. *Approaches to Religion and Mythology in Celtic studies.* Newcastle upon Tyne: Cambridge Scholars Publishing.

Ritchie, Graham and Anna. 1991. *Scotland: Archaeology and Early History.* Edinburgh: University of Edinburgh Press.

Rolfe, John C. 1939. *Ammianus Marcellinus.* Loeb Classical Library. Cambridge: Harvard University Press.

Ross, Anne. 1996. *Pagan Celtic Britain.* Chicago: Academy.

Sailer, Susan Shaw. 1997. "Leaps, Curses and Flight: Suibne Geilt and the

Roots of Early Irish Culture." *Études Celtiques* 23: 191-208.

Schot, Roseanne. 2011. "From cult centre to royal centre: monuments, myths and other revelations at Uisneach." In *Landscapes of Cult and Kingship*, edited by Rosanne Schot, Conor Newman and Edel Bhreathnach, 87-113. Dublin: Four Courts Press.

Scowcroft, R. Mark. 1995. "Abstract Narrative in Ireland." *Ériu* 46:121-158.

Sims-Williams, Patrick. 1990. "Some Celtic otherworld Terms." In *Celtic Language, Celtic Culture: A Festschrift for Eric P. Hamp*. Edited by A.T.E. Matonis and Daniel Melia, 57-81. Van Nuys: Ford and Bailie.

Sjoblom, Tom. 2004. "Mind-Stories: A Cognitive Approach to the Role of Narratives in Early Irish Tradition." *Cambrian Medieval Celtic Studies* 47:59-72.

Sjoestedt, Marie-Louise. 1982. *Gods and Heroes of the Celts*. Berkeley: Turtle Island Foundation.

Stokes, Whitley. 1868. *Cormac's Glossary*. Calcutta: Irish Archaeological and Celtic Society.

Thomson, R.L. 2002. *Pwyll Pendeuic Dyuet*. Dublin: Dublin Institute for Advanced Studies.

Trevarthen, Geo A. 2003. *Brightness of Brightness: Seeing Celtic Shamanism*. PhD thesis, University of Edinburgh.

Vitebsky, Piers. 2001. *Shamanism*. Norman: University of Oklahoma Press.

Waddell, John. 2014. *Archaeology and Celtic Myth*. Dublin: Four Courts Press.

Watkins, Calvert. 2000. *Dictionary of Indo-European Roots*. Boston: Houghton Mifflin.

———— 1995. *How to Kill a Dragon*. Oxford: Oxford University Press.

Williams, Ifor. 1954. *Lectures on Early Welsh Poetry*. Dublin: Dublin Institute for Advanced Studies.

———— 1951. *Pedeir Keinc y Mabinogi*. Cardiff: University of Wales Press.

Withers, Charles W.J. and R.W. Munro, eds. 1999. *Martin Martin - A Description of the Western Islands of Scotland circa 1695*. Edinburgh: Birlinn.

Wooding, Jonathan. 2009. "Re-approaching the Pagan Celtic Past – Anti-Nativism, Asterisk Reality and the Late-Antiquity Paradigm." *Studia Celtica Fennica* 6:61-74.

———— 2000. *The Otherworld Voyage in Early Irish Literature: An Anthology*

PART 2

On Desmond Bell's "The Last Storyteller?" A Panel Discussion

DESMOND BELL, LOUISE S. MILNE, LIV WILLUMSEN

INTRODUCTION: NOTES ON THE LAST STORYTELLER

'The Last Storyteller' is an original film by director Des Bell which deals with the life of the renowned Irish folk lore collector Seán ÓhEochaidh. Seán began his work with the Irish Folk Lore Commission in 1935 and for the next forty years travelled the highways and byways of the remote Irish speaking areas of the northwest of Ireland recording the folklore and fairy tales of the last generation of traditional storytellers. The film recounts some of the engaging but uncanny stories ÓhEochaidh unearthed in his native Donegal. It interweaves interviews with ÓhEochaidh in the last years of his life, archival (found) footage of Irish rural life, and dramatic reconstructions: of ÓhEochaidh's life as a young collector, travelling throughout Gaeltaecht areas on his bike with his ediphone recording machine; and of the actual stories he collected. ÓhEochaidh died in January 2002 just as the film was completed. Bell employs an innovative use of archive footage that provides rich and evocative images of the people and the landscape that inspired the original tales. There are five stories in all, each one dealing in some way with ordinary mortals and their interaction with the 'other world', either good or bad. The collector asks one of his favourite respondents, an old woman, does she actually believe in the fairies. She answers, partly tongue in cheek, "It doesn't matter a bit whether I believe in the fairies or not... sure they're there anyway!" In the final tale, 'The Pig-Headed Child,' a traditional post-Famine Ireland story is dramatized into a contemporary tale of hubris and social exclusion in Celtic Tiger Ireland, suggesting the relevance of these tales to our lives today.

The other thread running through the film is provided by Walter Benjamin's famous essay 'The Storyteller in Artisan Culture' which so lucidly reflects on what is lost with the demise of oral culture and which was written the year after Seán began his work as a collector. This critical strand is interwoven with images of the crafts and occasions which supported the telling and sharing of stories. The film vividly dramatises a world already well on its way to disappearing between the wars and asks its viewers what is lost in our culture with the end of traditional storytelling. It also celebrates the narrative capacity of cinema itself suggesting that perhaps film take on the mantle of story-telling. The director, Desmond Bell, had already worked closely with ÓhEochaidh in the making of his award-winning film 'Hard Road to Klondike' (1990) another tale collected by ÓhEochaidh and eventually turned into a much-loved book with his help. In 'The Last Storyteller' Bell had the opportunity to acknowledge that debt and celebrate the tireless and inspired work of ÓhEochaidh.

The Last Storyteller. 2002 colour/ black and white. 52 mins. Broadcast RTE television March 2002, selected for the Venice International Film Festival. Written and directed by Desmond Bell. Produced by Margo Harkin for Besom Productions.

DISCUSSION

Edited transcript of a panel discussion between Louise Milne (LM), Liv Willumsen (LW) and Desmond Bell (DB), chaired by Margaret MacKay, organised by the Institute for Advanced Studies in the Humanities at the University of Edinburgh, held in Edinburgh on Friday 17th February 2016.

Chair: This film raises interesting questions and angles for us about the nature of oral transmission, the content and role of tales in the past and in the present, the nature of technique and the way in which approaches, different approaches to a variety of media can help in an understanding of art forms and an expression of creativity; lots of material here for us. And to help us in our discussion today, along with Desmond Bell, the film writer and director, we have first Dr Louise Milne, historian, visual anthropologist and filmmaker (University of Edinburgh and Edinburgh Napier University). Louise will set the scene from the perspective of her disciplines.

LM: Well, there are some key issues that are brought into focus and framed by this excellent film. The first one is to do with film itself and the second one is to do with the subject, of storytelling and folk beliefs. The connection between the two is the issue of recording, I think, and in particular the question of time. If you look at this film as a filmmaker, you'll see that Des has carefully woven together a number of strands, visual strands, visual codes to the film. The most obvious one perhaps is the archive footage, which comes from many different places but which is changed, shifted into black and white or a CGI element brought in. It shifts between black and white and colour throughout the film, and colourisation is used also to indicate a kind of magical embeddedness of these beliefs in the actual life world of the people. And I think this is a really interesting way of approaching the whole subject. In the underwater scenes, the landscape photography and the changes of speed–you will have noticed perhaps the shots of the waterfall and of the clouds meeting over the west coast landscapes–all of this gives a great sense of time, many different kinds of time, actually embedded in the film, and absolutely paralleled in the content of the material, if we think about the stories, how old they are, how they are used, whether they are throwaway lines like "away with the fairies" or longer, more epic elements. This is particularly clear in the beautiful and moving use of the World War II footage, matched with the Irish version of the story of War in Heaven, given a lyrical turn and woven into indigenous beliefs about the fairies in the idea of angels falling as the bombs fall. Now the viewer knows perfectly well that we are not seeing little people, devils falling from heaven during creation, and yet the analogy is fantastic, underwritten also when the film returns, after the fall of the rebel angels, to the World War II context with the bombing of Belfast and the banshee that was heard the night before. I love that interrelationship. The film provides many different dramatizations of how our hero recorded these tales. We hear the subject's own voice. We hear a dramatised voice in sweeping middle age, the voice of the actor, Stephen Green, the narrator, reflecting on this biographical journey: "I'd heard so many tales about the fairies and almost to the point of hearing them myself. Wouldn't you?"

The idea that stories are embedded in work is Walter Benjamin's great insight: they are embedded in collective work, they are an oral art form. They can have a palliative function in managing issues of luck, as in the story of the red fox with which we start, which takes the form of a *memorate*, a story told in the first person: this really happened to me, this happened to my neighbour. The film gives us a sense of the variety of uses of this collective oral culture, this culture of the imagination, how it is interwoven with everyday life, with particular traditional trades and tasks spinning everything in a web. It is indeed a web, as Benjamin and Delaney say, through which people make sense of the world, and also reflect and make art in the imaginative sense.

Chair: Thank you Louise. Now, we hear from Liv Willumsen, here at IASH for several months from the University of Tromso in Norway. She is a professor in the history department there, and she has a particular interest which draws her to Scotland and Scottish material, and that is witchcraft. She's worked, edited and researched the story of witch trials in Norway, particularly in north Norway, very extensively and this, for various reasons, has brought her to Scottish evidence as well, as Scots themselves were involved in those witch trials to some extent. She has been a researcher and scholar of the Scottish witch trials too. So she brings a different perspective to this film.

LW: Thank you very much, Maggie. I would say that I received *The Last Storyteller* as a beautiful film about ÓhEochaidh and his life as a collector of folklore, and a man with the greatest respect for the art of storytelling and the art of listening. My first interest in the interpretation of the film is that, as a literary scholar, I have worked much with narrative structures of text, narrative structures of stories. So I would like to comment on two clear strings of the film which I see are related in an interesting way in the structure of the film. And there I come very close to some points already discussed. One string is ÓhEochaidh's life story, his boyhood, his work in the fishing boat, his start in collecting stories in 1935, and his lifelong work as a folklorist, as a collector of stories. From this perspective the film has a timeline. For instance, he mentions both his father and grandfather, and they have a place in this timeline. The other string I can see is thematically-based. It consists of the stories, one story after another, like embedded narratives in this timeline of his life. And these embedded narratives contain themes of various kinds, from the story of the fisherman finding the boy, then the omen of the fox and the shark, the girl selling milk and the sailor kissing her apron, and the fairy lore that we see unfolding. When ÓhEochaidh comes to this mountainous area in 1939 he finds genuine storytellers as informants and very old people also as informants. This is an area where storytelling is created.

What fascinates me most in this part of his life as storyteller is the fairy lore. It is there in the tale about the pig-headed child at the end with the woman who was the daughter of the queen. It is also there in the tale of the widow and the fairy girl, and in the one about the cobbler, his wife and the changeling, where we also find the motif of the changeling, in which the fairies replace the real living human figure of flesh and blood with one of their own. These embedded narratives, as they are shown in the film one after another, they tell us both of his life, of his insight and his understanding.

There is a movement in ÓhEochaidh's own life following the movement of the stories he is collecting. It goes towards a darker and more dangerous stage, particularly when the word of fairies, and their power comes to the fore in the stories told by the old genuine storytellers. Here we go deeper into the impact of the otherworld and its forces. Thus also the reference to the grandfather: notice that this connection to the previous generation is also aligned with the fairy lore. What interests me–and this is something I saw several times in witchcraft trial confessions–is the moment, in the fairy lore of Scotland and Ireland, when you are able to trust this very, very thin border between our world and the next world. Scottish and Irish folklore explains and presents the world of the fairies in different ways than Norwegian folklore; there, the fairies are much less dangerous, they are not so wild, they are much smaller and more elegant things; and they do not have this very strong force that you see in the material from Scotland and Ireland.

So I have three questions that I hope Desmond could answer, or others in the audience. The first one is, for what reasons, Desmond, among all the stories that ÓhEochaidh collected, did you select the stories that are told in the film? And second, how do the stories told in the film relate to ÓhEochaidh's own life and insight? This must have something to do his taking in of the otherworld, what he experienced when he came to this mountainous area and suddenly saw a much more genuine type of folklore due to the closed place and the very isolated living conditions. And the last question I would like to ask: what are grounds for choosing archival material when telling the first stories and then using more modern tools when presenting the last story of the pig-headed child? Do we here see something of the question mark of the film's title, that ÓhEochaidh's stories will be told again by new narrators but in a new setting and in a new mould?

DB: Well, let us start with the question of the selection of the stories. Although I'm familiar with this part of the world and was very familiar with Seán ÓhEochaidh – I worked with him on a previous film (*Rotha Mor an tSaiol*, or the Big Wheel of Life; the English title was *Hard Road to Klondike*), I am a rather hard-bitten historical materialist when it comes to life, and the world of folklore was not naturally an area that I would have been attracted to. But the stories that I selected and the way they were interpreted are indebted to someone like Angela Carter. I'm not a folklorist, I was interested in these as indexes of social contradictions in Irish society, contradictions which manifest themselves in very elliptical ways historically in stories. The science of folklore collection is not really interested in those issues: it is predominately interested in a taxonomy of folk tales rather a social interpretation of them. And the great virtue of trying to work with the Walter Benjamin material was that Benjamin is trying to identify the decline of storytelling against the backdrop of the transition from an artisan world to an industrial economy. Therefore how can storytelling be preserved? And of course this is a film. And to Benjamin the answer would be simple: storytelling is preserved in film. Film is reflexive in the sense that it attempts to show how both the assemblage of archive material and the live action drama are contemporary forms of storytelling. This point is made towards the end of the film. The particular selection of the stories depends also on pragmatic concerns, on what can be told on film. Many of the stories are long and complicated, therefore questions on the economy of the storytelling became important. Secondly, I considered what I could illuminate and illustrate with the archive I had. And to some extent also I discussed the issue with ÓhEochaidh, in terms of what were his favourite stories. Most of them came from the collection on South Donegal that he edited. So they came from that source and were tweaked a little bit, of course, to get the fit between the archive and the dialogue... and your the other question?

LW: The other was what could be the connection between the themes, the contents of the stories and his own life as he's going into an elderly period of his life, and then meeting this very deep material of the fairy lore?

DB: Well, the fairy stories that he collected, and the transition in our film that you identify, when he goes into the Blue Stack Mountains above Ardera, that was the last monoglot area of Irish speaking in Ireland, and for that reason particular respondents that he had there, the MacAloon family and Mara MacAloon and Noon MacAloon, he regarded these as the real genuine article, people who had reworked their stories in two or three generations, honed them to a fine skill within the Irish language, up to that point not particularly influenced by Anglophonic traditions... And it has to be borne in mind, during this period, the Second World War, mobility in Ireland was really quite difficult, so this was a secluded area which became even more secluded for those years. Up until the 1960s it really was a land apart. So yes, there is a sense in which he's going into that area. The other theme I always wanted to bring into it was his endless talking about the collapse of storytelling, which he identified with the end of cèilidh as a tradition and particularly the arrival of the television. It was the television, he said, that killed cèilidh. And also certain new social norms developed, about dropping into people's houses. The whole point about cèilidh was that you were not invited, people just went round in an entourage round to various houses at certain nights of the week; it was an open house system. Once people departed from that, and the bourgeois delicacies of invitations and all the rest came into play, together with television, which led to the privatisation of social activity, that was the end of storytelling. It was not possible to tell that sociological story within the film, except for a hint towards the end, in the urban scenes of Dublin. [When I was making the film] this was the height of the Celtic boom, and also the height of Roma people arriving into the city for the first time; a modern contemporary migration crisis manifesting itself in Ireland. People were already drawing parallels to the displacements that had occurred in Ireland after the famine. The Lady Gregory song and the Pig Head tale form a story about rural displacement after the famine, not completely removed from the sort of displacements occurring across Europe at the moment. That final section of the film was an attempt to try and bring these things to some form of alignment, at the same time showing that this world of Dublin and the Celtic boom was a world that ÓhEochaidh could never have comprehended. He was aware of it, this was a man who travelled to Dublin regularly, who collected in South Uist, who knew Scotland well, who had visited London and many countries. But changes had taken place, and the age he was living in had passed him by, so there is sense in which there is a transition towards the end of the film towards accepting. That's the second one. I will add something myself, then. There are ethical issues that anybody that conducts an ethnography wrestles with. I was not considering ethnography as such, I was taking existing material and retelling stories. Yes, I think there is a difference clearly between film-making and the sort of exchange that ÓhEochaidh saw himself as involved in. He used to always say that he always had to take something for his storytellers, even if it was only a little bit of tobacco or a little sugar–during the war these things were very scarce–so there was a sense of reciprocity and exchange. He was aware that something changed significantly when he moved from just being a fisherman sharing stories. He was the only collector who was not a professional or a professionally educated person; the majority of them were national school teachers. He had not been to secondary school, he had left school at 14. Seamus Delarcey was really taking a chance to some extent with ÓhEochaidh: would Seán be able to do the job, to meet the bureaucratic requirements of the Folklore Commission? Certainly ÓhEochaidh realised that he made a transition which he was often uncomfortable with, from talking to people as equals to talking to people as a collector, which was to impose his set of structures on the relationship. And he saw that, by the giving of gifts and the swapping of stories and information, when the edit-phone was turned off; he reported that as a problem. Now I think within folklore collection there was no real awareness of those ethnographic dilemmas. I do not see it in any of the fieldwork notes.

LM: I think that is the whole point of the final episode; that is what it is there for. You have to remember that film is intrinsically a distancing device, it has absolutely engrained in it the Cartesian perspectival model of distance. Film-makers have always dealt with this issue, of framing, putting people in boxes; the question of the stare, of intrusion and so on, especially in documentary making. I thought that the real unease, the difficulty, the mismatch in the film comes in the concept of the Pig-Headed Child story and the way that it is dramatized in this sort of elusive postmodern way; but the end is not magical but tragic. I thought that that was a way of resolving and squaring that circle.

DB: I'll tell you a story, about this business of encapsulating a life in film material. I was cutting the film with Roger Buck, an excellent editor who has just recently retired from Napier. In the section when Seán goes into the mountains, we show a family in the field collecting something. I said to Roger or Roger said to me: 'What are those? They don't look like potatoes.' Roger was trained as an agricultural economist, so he had some interest in this. We could not work it out. It did not seem to be lazy beds, as potatoes would have been grown in Donegal in that period. About seven years later I was showing the film at an event in Galway, and I told the story about Roger. I said, 'These editors, they can't focus on the job, they get off on all sorts of red herrings.' And a little hand went up in the back and said, 'Cabbages.' I said, 'Sorry?' 'Cabbages. That was me.' This woman was now in her seventies, the piece of film was shot by Welsh ethnographic students in 1947 and she had, probably for the first time ever, now seen herself in this. The archive footage is in the Welsh film archive, and she would have no access to it. It was well understood at the time that all these stories were being collected within a project of public culture, but it was not available. It was available in principle, but in practice, because of the technologies, people did not hear the stories. And most of the recordings were not kept, most of the wax cylinders were erased and transcribed over the years. The fieldwork notes were all kept and that is the basis of the collection, along with the transcriptions. There definitely was an understanding that this was part of a national task and that was very clearly communicated in setting up the Folklore Commission. And whoever gave their testaments, their stories, did so with the understanding that this was a worthwhile activity, in a public cultural context.

LM: What about the Pig-Headed Child story? Can you say some more on that?

DB: The Pig-Headed Child is a story about perceived disability, and the inability, in Irish culture, up until very recently, to deal with the question of disability. I think that aspect is in the original story, and to some extent also in how we told it. The whole idea is that when the Pig-Headed Child is born she cannot be allowed out, she has to keep in in case anybody saw her. This was the reality of disability and how disability was dealt with in families up until about 20 years ago, 30 years ago perhaps, in Ireland. So there are hints and suggestions at that in the original story, I think. As in all the stories there is a social text to be read in the narrative. We attempted, without being too over-interpretive, to read some of this into the stories.

Audience member: This is a question really for all of you on the panel, to do with the nature of these stories. We are living now in a world where, even in the most remote, the most rural areas of places like Ireland and Scotland, even in places where traditions have remained relatively intact compared to the rest of these countries, economic and cultural and material situations have changed utterly. What role can these particular stories then, the stories from that time and that set of circumstances, rather than just stories in general, continue to have? Can it be something more than nostalgia?

LM: Of course it is more than nostalgia. I do not personally think that these stories were told always told with a purpose or a moral, although one might be attached to them, possibly, as with the changeling motif. But then, the idea of the changeling in itself has a sort of attractive identity, it is good to think with, it is multivalent, polysemic. There is a sort of paradox, a problem here as to how old this material was. You say these stories date from the famine. In other words, they are not generations old, they are not from the dawn of time. They are in fact a constantly evolving stream, and this is an important aspect of folklore. It is a question of whether or not we are interested in getting at this illusory idea of an elusive time, when all of this was whole and completely authentic: arguably, it never could have been. The reason stories stay the same for generations is because the material culture and way of life stays the same. The minute that changes, the stories will change too, this must always have happened. The interesting thing really is how much of that storytelling technique survives, applied to things which are no longer to do with spinning and fishing. There is an entire world of modern legend and modern tales, about the devil at the disco and so on. And since all of this is ongoing, we can assume it's ongoing in Ireland and Scotland too.

LW: I would like to add some thoughts. If you go to a deep thematic understanding of the stories there is not only the question of understanding the materialistic basis: the way or means people have to earn their living or to manage to go on with their life. There is much more a kind of understanding of what life is, on the thematic level. Why are we, and I guess you are also in Scotland and Ireland, still celebrating Midsummer Eve? Midwinter eve? We mark these days of the year even today. It is not a long time ago, it is not nostalgia: we are still celebrating these days because the year is turning around. Long before Christian times, the year is turning to another period, of life, types of life or types of temperature. And on these special days of the year we say in Norway, 'This border between our world and the other world can be passed,' and we see people from the otherworld come in, like the red haired children in the film. It has to do with an understanding of life and environment, that maybe there is something more around that we do not see. This is not superstition, it's a feeling towards life. And this is why I ask, what about ÓhEochaidh himself as an elderly man, going into different phases of story collecting? What happened to him? What did he see? What did he understand? When he went into this period of his life when he really met the genuine storyteller, what did they have to reveal to him? This is also the core, why these stories are not outdated, the stories still have a core meaning that could be retold in our days.

DB: The capacity to narrativise experience does appear to be diminished. One is very reluctant to make an absolute judgement on that because it is a wee bit early to really assess what the impact of digitalisation and social media are. But it appears to be the case that our perception of time, notions of continuity, notions of social and community integrity, those things do rest upon a capacity to narrativise things. And with our capacity of narrativise apparently diminished, there is atomisation that is occurring in society. I do not think I'm announcing a thesis that people have not heard, I think that is the case. Now of course film making and film culture emerged at the threshold of industrial modernity, and in America, which was a society in which that atomisation proceeded very quickly, with the melting pot. Filmmaking and film language did provide a way of storytelling. The other thing about the mystery of film as it presented itself, particularly silent films for those who would see them for the first time, is that they must have appeared pretty magical. I mean literally film replaced magic: it is about action at a distance, it is about the relation between space and time, which are much closer to the things that take place in the fairy story to anything that you are going to see in the street outside the theatre. There is a sense in which the film medium itself is not just a continuation of storytelling, it is a continuation of magical storytelling, a certain transcendence from the quotidian in all sorts of ways, that is how people saw early cinema. The reason I have always been fascinated with the use of archival footage is the magic of the archive, the magic of the filmmaking process. It seems to me not a million miles away from the fascination of the fairies.

Desmond Bell is a filmmaker working in the field of creative documentary. He is also Professor and Head of Academic Affairs at the National College of Art and Design in Dublin, where he runs the PhD programme and is Director of Research.

Margaret Mackay is University lecturer and was Director of the School of Scottish Studies Archives at the University of Edinburgh, where she is currently Honorary Fellow of the department of Celtic and Scottish Studies.

Louise S. Milne is an historian, visual anthropologist and film-maker. She teaches at the University of Edinburgh and at Edinburgh Napier University. She is the author of Carnivals and Dreams: Pieter Bruegel and the History of the Imagination.

Liv Helene Willumsen is Professor at the Institutt for arkeologi, historie, religionsvitenskap og teologi at UiT Norges Arktiske Universitet, Tromsø, Norway.

PART 3

Reviews

Stories of the Sea: Maritime Memorates of Ireland and Scotland, by Maxim Fomin and Séamus Mac Mathúna (in collaboration with John Shaw and Criostóir Mac Carthaigh; assisted by Séamus Mac Floinn). Berlin: Currach Bhán Publications, 2016. ISBN 978-3-942002-16-5, € 19.90, 83 pages.

Born out of a three-year research project, this well-produced volume presents an array of preliminary findings and collected materials gathered under the rubric "Stories of the Sea: A typological study of maritime memorates in modern Irish and Scottish Gaelic folklore traditions." The original project involved close collaboration with the National Folklore Collection at University College Dublin and the School of Scottish Studies archives at the University of Edinburgh. The publication also received support from the Arts and Humanities Council and Ulster University.

The time period under investigation extends from the middle of the nineteenth century to the present day, and the book includes a selection of first-hand personal accounts of experiences at sea by Irish and Scottish fisherman, boatmen and shore gatherers. Where possible, narratives are first given in modern Irish or Scottish Gaelic, with an English translation provided.

Recollections of supernatural encounters and events are an important component of the narrative traditions of coastal communities in both Ireland and Scotland. The study aims to contribute to a greater understanding of the social and cultural life of these communities, and the close maritime connections between Ireland and Scotland over the centuries.

The book is divided into two main sections, one containing stories from Ireland, and one stories from Scotland. The collection also includes archival photographs pertaining to the stories at hand, such as pictures of fisherman, maritime crafts, and the recording of traditional bearers. Several illustrations are also present, including images taken from the notebooks of folklore collectors, maps, and useful notes. All in all, *Stories of the Sea* constitutes an excellent addition to the corpus of publications about folklore narratives and traditional communities.

Sharon Paice MacLeod

The Power of Words: Studies on Charms and Charming in Europe, by James Kapaló, Éva Pócs, and William Ryan, eds. Budapest and New York: Central European University Press, 2013. ISBN 978-615-5225-10-9, £45, 334 pages.

An edited collection of scholarly articles dealing with charms, charm-making and charm-collecting across various European contexts, *The Power of Words* offers an original, well structured contribution to the field. The internal organisation of the volume follows a clear tripartition, with the main sections described as 1) Genre, Classification and Terminology; 2) Historical and Comparative Studies; and 3) Content and Function of Charms. Several traditions are considered across the volume, with charms originating from Norway, Scotland, England, Portugal, Finland, Hungary, Romania, and Baltic and Slavic regions. Some essays employ a more broad-based approach, examining medieval charms, charm indexes, and charm terminology, as examples.

In Part One, Arne Bugge Amundsen provides an introduction to the first study of charms in Norway. This is followed by an in-depth and fascinating account of 'the making of a charm collector,' relating to the notable work of Alexander Carmichael, specifically in Uist between 1864 and 1882. This essay provides a great deal of unpublished material pertaining to the conditions and intentions of Carmichael's work, as well as the varied responses and attitudes of his informants. Tatiana Agapkina and Andrei Toporkov explore problems and perspectives pertaining to charm indexes, a useful essay for students of folklore. Edina Bozóky discusses written medieval narrative charms, and Vilmos Voigt provides information on the historical development of Hungarian charm terminology.

In Part Two, Lea Olsan's essay explores the marginality of charms in medieval England, followed by Éva Pócs' interesting article on church benedictions and popular charms in Hungary. Especially remarkable in her contribution were the sections on magical and religious commands, enumerations and similes, the use of religious texts as amulets, and the use of charms for benediction and exorcism. The topic of benediction and exorcism in early modern Hungary is taken up by Dániel Bárth, followed by an exploration of Baltic and East Slavic charms by Daiva Vaitkeviciene.

In Part Three, Emanuela Timotin discusses Romanian charms that are intended to treat disease, including evidence from the manuscript tradition. Francisco Vaz Da Silva provides us with insights into moon charms for sick children in Portuguese ethnography, and Maarit Viljakainen discusses the invocation of the Virgin Mary in Finnish and Karelian birth incantations. Gábor Klaniczay provides the final essay in the work, exploring the power of words in relation to miracles, incantations and bewitchment, including vows and healing words.

The book is well-researched and well-written throughout, and provides ample material for the interested reader, as it explores several European folklore settings, from medieval through early modern times. An excellent resource for the student or researcher of charms and charming, both in European and other folklore contexts.

Sharon Paice MacLeod

Le Chaudron du Dagda, by Valéry Raydon. Marseilles: Terre de Promesse. ISBN 978-2-9541625-4-6, € 20, 174 pages.

The French historian and author Valéry Raydon discusses in depth the varied symbolism of the Irish deity known as *An Dagda* (The Dagda, the 'Good or Best God'), through an exploration of medieval Irish literature, including sagas and place-name lore, including comparisons with Gaulish and other Indo-European materials.

In Chapter One of *Le Chaudron du Dagda*, Raydon discusses the Four Talismans of the Túatha Dé Danann, as presented in *Cath Maige Tuired* and *Lebor Gabála Érenn*, including the relationship between the texts and the attributes they describe in relation to the talismans. Raydon outlines how the talismans may fulfill various symbolic functions, and in doing so he borrows prominently from Georges Dumézil's tripartite model. Of particular interest is the possibility that the cauldron may have been associated with feasts held at the four Irish seasonal festivals.

In Chapter Two, Raydon explores a variety of symbols associated with the Dagda, including his club, which wielded life from one end, and death from the other. He compares this with Continental representations of the deity Succelos, and explores terminology associated with the clubs or hammers of these gods as potentially related to branches originating in the Otherworld, or symbols of the world tree. The possibility that the Dagda may have had a connection with the sacred passage of time appears especially intriguing.

Chapter Three explores possible analogies between cauldrons possessed by deities or supernatural figures, and those possessed by kings or noble persons and used in royal or sacral feasts. It is one of the strongest sections of the book, and one that deserves further study. Raydon discusses the possible connection between the deity's club and meat forks used in conjunction with large cooking vessels during feasts and seasonal gatherings, and the concept of the 'Prince's Truth', which was, in some instances, also associated with various types of vessels.

The connection between supernatural cauldrons and those used at feasts hosted by kings or noblemen is further explored to good effect in Chapter Four, with a strong discussion of the redistribution of wealth or abundance. The chapter also explores interesting aspects of another of the Dagda's possessions, a magical harp, and its association with seasonal celebrations.

Chapter Five is concerned with hagiographical materials associated with several Irish saints, including Brigid and Moling. Brigid's connection with abundance is well documented, and Raydon adroitly explores episodes in which she is either connected with vessels of abundance, or in which she embodies that attribute directly within her own person. Saint Moling and the theme of cooking horse meat in a cauldron on the one hand, and representations of the rites of Sovereignty on the other, combine here to form an interesting argument in relation to Christian interdictions against the eating of horse meat as a 'pagan' activity.

Finally, in Chapter Six, the author discusses a wide variety of cauldrons, vessels, tubs, pools and bags – including the *corr-bolg* of the deity Manannán mac Lir – and a possible connection between the Dagda's cauldron with marine or Underworld symbolism, whirlpools, and the flooding of major Irish rivers. This last section is harder to follow than previous ones, but it still offers a great deal of material for consideration.

The book is clearly written, and holds the reader's interest throughout. There are a number of places where the author is perhaps too eager to equate one piece of evidence with another, and assert the antiquity of the themes he explores. However, he presents these connections as possible symbolic resonances, to delve further into the possible mythological strata at hand. A few errors crept in here and there, as in Chapter Two when the Irish name *Eochu* (earlier form *Echu*) is said to derive from a Celtic word meaning 'yew' (it is believed to derive from Old Irish *ech* 'horse'), or when Raydon proposes that large tribal gatherings were held on all four of the early Irish feast days (there is very little evidence for the observance of Imbolc in earlier sources, or on a large social scale).

The work would have benefited in places from more recent translations and commentaries. These may or may not impact the author's primary argument overall, but would help lay a solid foundation for his theories. It would have been interesting to explore the connection between the goddess *Bríg* and her father, the Dagda, in light of some of the themes discussed here. Indeed, a number of sections were ripe for further exploration, including the fascinating analogies between Otherworldly and festal cauldrons, other aspects of feasting (such as the music played by the Dagda's harp), and the role that other Irish deities may have played in relation to the prevalent themes of abundance and sovereignty. These faults notwithstanding, the book provides much food for thought, in relation to both Celtic materials and other Indo-European sources.

(Sharon Paice MacLeod)

DOSSIER

TWO RESPONSES TO JAMES MALLORY'S *IRISH DREAMTIME*

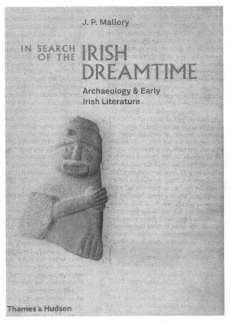

Irish Dreamtime. Archaeology & Early Irish Literature, by James P. Mallory. London: Thames & Hudson, 2016. ISBN 978-0-500-05184-9, £18.95, 320 pages.

RESPONSE 1

The book represents a unique attempt to confront the Irish mythic pseudo-history with results of modern archaeology. The author, James P. Mallory, is more than perfectly prepared for this task. He is an active and renowned archaeologist, operating not just in Irish Studies; he is also a respected comparative linguist and no less regarded as a specialist in comparative mythology. The present monograph was preceded by a series of special studies (Mallory 1981, 1984a, 1984b, 1986, 1987, 1988, 1990, 1991, 1992, 1993, 1994, 1995a, 1995b, 1996, 1997, 1998a, 1998b, 1999, 2002, 2004, 2006, 2009, 2013; with G.L. Baillie 1999). The term 'dreamtime' was deliberately chosen by the author through analogy to the same term used about the mythic past by Australian Aboriginals. In Australia, it refers especially to orally recorded tales and paintings, while in Ireland Mallory thinks of it as denoting the preliterary pseudo-history, recorded in the series of medieval texts, forming specific cycles. The main sources depicting the Irish 'dreamtime' are as follows (19-21):

1 The mythological cycle describing the earliest settlement, finishing around 100 BCE: *Lebor Gabála Érenn* 'Book of the Taking {Invasions} of Ireland', *Cét-chath Maige Tuired* 'First Battle of Mag Tuired', *Cath Tánaiste Maige Tuired* 'Second Battle of Mag Tuired'.
2 The Ulster cycle, with its central tale *Táin Bó Cuailnge* 'Cattle-raid of Cooley', preserved in three different recensions. The events it desribes are datable from *c.* 100 BCE to *c.* 400 CE.
3 The Finn or Osiannic cycle.
4 The Kings cycle.

The author adds other important sources of inspiration for the medieval Irish annalists, originating outside of Ireland (274):

5 Bible in Latin translation.
6 Roman authors writing in Latin, namely (68) Virgil, Ovid, Lucan, Statius, etc., Irish translations of which existed already in the twelfth century or earlier (with the exception of Ovid).
7 *Etymologiae* of Isidore of Seville.

The most valuable result of the book is a comparative overview of two sets of chronologies: one in which remarkable events are dated by annalists, and one in which the same events are matched to their impact on material culture, which in turn can be dated through archaeological methods (see Table 1).

It becomes apparent, then, that in only a few cases the two sets of datings appear to match, and those are limited to brewing, pointed metal spears, gold, smelted gold, gold chains, gold rings, and maybe Dún Ailinne: in total 5-7 items out of 29. The dominant role of gold in this partial list is remarkable.

By contrast, the two sets of datings display a higher rate of overlapping in relation to demographic catastrophes (e.g. 'plague') or sudden cattle mortality, where annalistic data can be matched to dendrological evidence such as narrow annual rings and, relatedly, eruptions of volcanos from Iceland or Mediterranean (Table 2).

Event	Annalistic Dating	Archaeological Dating	Discrepancy
Initial settlement	3000 BCE	8000 BCE	+5000 years
First livestock	3000 BCE	3800 BCE	+800
First land clearance	2700 BCE	3800 BCE	+1100
First cairns	3000 BCE	3800 BCE	+800
Guesting house	2700 BCE	3800 BCE	+1000
Cauldrons	2700 BCE	1200 BCE	-1500
Brewing	2700 BCE	2500 BCE	-200
Ploughing	2700 BCE	3800 BCE	+1100
Querns	2700 BCE	3800 BCE	+1100
Dairy products	2700 BCE	3600 BCE	+900
Gold	2700 BCE	2300 BCE	-400
Forts	2400 BCE	3800/1000 BCE	+1400/ -1400
Pointed (metal) spears	1900 BCE	1700 BCE	-200
Silver	1700 BCE	100 BCE	-1600
Swords	1700 BCE	1200 BCE	-500
Board games	1700 BCE	100 BCE	-1600
Chariots	1700 BCE	300 BCE	-1400
Horse (racing)	1700 BCE	1000 BCE	-700
Tara's wall	1700 BCE	100 BCE	-1600
Gold smelted (cast)	1500 BCE	2000/1400-1100 BCE	+500 or -100

Gold vessels	1500 BCE	300 BCE / 700 CE	-1200 or -2200
Silver vessels	1500 BCE	700 CE	-2200
Gold brooches	1500 BCE	1000 BCE / 700 CE	-500 or -2200
Silver brooches	1500 BCE	700 CE	-2200
Silver shields	1400 BCE	(silver) 100 BCE	-1300
Gold chains	1300 BCE	1300 BCE	0
Gold rings	1300 BCE	1300 BCE	0
Ditch of Emain Macha	700-300 BCE	100 BCE	-600 / -200
Dún Ailinne	1000 BCE? / 100 BCE	100 BCE	-900 or 0

Table 1. Chronologies compared. Source: Mallory 2016, 98.

Event	Annalistic Dating	Dendrological Dating	Correlated Event
9,000 people die within one week	2382-2350 BCE	2345 BCE	Eruption of Hekla 4
Three-quarters of the men of Ireland die	1620-1544 BCE	1628 BCE	Eruption of Santorini
Countless numbers die in plague	1180-1031 BCE	1159 BCE	Eruption of Hekla 3
Great mortality of cattle	209-199 BCE	207 BCE	?

Table 2. Chronologies compared (natural disasters). Source: Mallory 2016, 94.

The book is also very carefully prepared, there are practically no misprints or mistakes. One exception is the Greek word ξίφος "sword", transcribed here as *zíphos* (65), whereas the correct transliteration would be *ksíphos*.

In any case, the present monograph represents a successful continuation of Mallory's preceding offering, *The Origins of the Irish* (2013). Both illustrate the possibilities in combining several disciplines to map the early past of Ireland. This approach is clearly applicable to other territories.

Václav Blažek

Reference

Mallory, James P. 1981. "The Sword of the Ulster Cycle." In *Studies on Early Ireland: Essays in honour of M.V. Duignan*, edited by B.G. Scott, 99-114. Belfast: Association of Young Irish Archaeologists.

———— 1984a. *Navan Fort: The Ancient Capital of Ulster*. Belfast: Ulster Archaeological Society.

———— 1984b. "The Origins of the Irish." *Journal of Irish Archaeology* 2: 65-69.

———— 1986. "Silver in the Ulster Cycle of Tales." In *Proceedings of the Seventh International Congress of Celtic Studies*, edited by D. Ellis Evans, John G. Griffith and E. M. Jope, 31-78. Oxford: Oxford University Press.

———— 1987. "The Literary Topography of Emain Macha." *Emania* 2: 12-18.

———— 1988. "A Provisional Checklist of Crúachain in the Annals." *Emania* 5: 24-26.

———— 1990. "Irish Early Iron Age Sites: A Provisional Map of Absolute Dated Sites." *Emania* 7: 46-50.

———— 1991. "Two Perspectives On Irish Origins." *Emania* 9: 53-58.

———— 1992. "The World of Cú Chulainn: The Archaeology of Táin Bó Cúailnge." In *Aspects of the Táin*, edited by James P. Mallory, 103-159. Belfast: December.

———— 1993. "Die Archaeologie der Táin". In *Scriptoralia*, edited by H. L. C. Tristram, 192-230. Freiburg.

———— 1994. "The Fort of the Ulster Tales." *Emania* 12: 28-38.

———— 1995a. "Haughey's Fort: Macha's Other Twin." *Archaeology Ireland* 9: 28-30.

———— 1995b. "The Archaeology of the Irish Dreamtime." In *Proceedings of the Harvard Celtic Colloquium 13: 1993*, edited by Barbara Hillers, Pamela Hopkins and Jerry Hunter, 1-24. Cambridge: Harvard University Press.

———— 1996. s.v. "Emain Macha"; "New Grange." *The Oxford Companion to Irish Literature*, edited by Robert Welch, 171-172; 391. Oxford: Clarendon Press.

———— 1997. "Emain Macha and Navan Fort," in *Excavations at Navan Fort 1961-71*, edited by C. J. Lynn, 197-207. Belfast: The Stationery Office.

———— 1998a. "The Old Irish chariot." In *Mír Curad: Studies in Honor of Calvert Watkins*, edited by J. Jasanoff, H. Melchert, and L. Oliver, 451-464. Innsbruck: Innsbrucker Beitrage zur Sprachwissenschaft.

———— 1998b. "The Origins of the Population of Ireland: A Survey of Putative Immigrations in Irish Prehistory and History." *Emania* 17: 47-81.

———— 1999. "Language in Orehistoric Ireland." *Ulster Folklife* 45: 3-16.

———— 2002. "Recent Excavations and Speculations on the Navan complex." *Antiquity* 76: 532-541.

———— 2004. "Emain Macha." In vol. 1 of *Encyclopedia of Irish History and Culture*, edited by J. Donnelly, 214. Detroit: Thomson Gale.

———— 2006. "Irish Origins: The Archaeological, Linguistic and Genetic Evidence." In *Migration and Myth: Ulster's Revolving Door*, edited by B. S. Turner, 97-111. Downpatrick: Ulster Local History Trust.

———— 2009. "The Conundrum of Iron Age Ceramics: the Evidence of Language." In *Relics in Old Decency: Archaeological Studies in Later Prehistory. Festschrift for Barry Raftery*, edited by Gabriel Cooney et al., 181-192. Dublin: Wordwell.

———— 2013. *The Origins of the Irish*. London: Thames & Hudson.

Mallory, James P. and G. L. Baillie. 1999. "Dating Navan Fort." *Antiquity* 73: 427-431.

RESPONSE 2

J.P Mallory is Emeritus Professor of Prehistoric Archaeology at Queen's University Belfast, well-known for his many contributions to the field of Irish and Indo-European studies, including *In Search of the Indo-Europeans* and *The Origins of the Irish*. With *In Search of the Irish Dreamtime*, Mallory provides us with a well-researched and highly readable work, and a fascinating journey through history, pre-history and mythology. He explores a wide range of written sources from medieval Ireland, and compares the world depicted in these sources with relevant archaeological records. The sources constitute a diverse array of recorded Irish histories, dating back to prehistory and including annals, ethnographic commentaries, sagas and narratives, many of which have long been established in the mythological corpus of the Irish tradition.

In Chapter One, 'Discovering the Earliest Irish Tradition,' Mallory guides the reader through the labyrinthine development of these sources, including Gerald of Wales' *The History and Topography of Ireland, Lebor Gabála Érenn*, and the *Annals of the Four Masters*, and addresses themes of chronology, historicity and synthesis. In Chapter Two, 'Impossible Stories and Impertinent Tales,' he proposes to try and align events described in the Mythological Cycle and the Ulster Cycle with dates outlined in the *Annals of the Four Masters* and *Lebor Gabála*. This chapter is quite dense: the discussion proceeds rapidly, offering an inundation of information about early Irish writings dealing with the mythic past, and how those might theoretically align with the pseudo-histories of the medieval period.

In Chapter Three, 'Excavating the Dreamtime,' Mallory explores themes such as authorship, storytelling and the oral tradition, verse versus prose, and literary archaeology, setting the stage for much of what follows. Chapter Four, 'The Archaeology of the Irish National Origin Legend,' attempts to compare the written record of *Lebor Gabála* and its attendant summaries in the *Annals of the Four Masters* with the archaeological records. This is an ambitious 'thought experiment,' as Mallory describes it, reaching back into prehistory and attempting to explore the synthetic materials in terms of time as well as space (the physical environment and the archaeological record).

Subsequent chapters follow the same pattern, comparing written materials with evidence from archaeology, each chapter treating a particular theme: the natural environment (landscape, flora and fauna), the built environment (including royal sites), warfare and weapons, transport, material culture, and burial. Mallory is at his strongest in these chapters, as he deftly sifts through a remarkable amount of literary and physical evidence. In many instances, he is able to clearly show how certain aspects of the physical and temporal world depicted in the written sources do not align with the evidence from archaeology. One of the most fascinating examples was the absence of long, slashing swords as described in narratives believed to depict events from the Iron Age, a time in which much shorter blades were in use in Ireland. In other instances, such as the presence of cauldrons or certain types of garments during many of the time periods under investigation, it is difficult to ascertain with precision to which period the items (or the events described) actually belong. These chapters contain many of the most important substantive materials under discussion, as Mallory attempts to assign each physical element to its proper time period. However, there are many areas of ambiguity, and ample room for the reader to make his or her own assessments (particularly in light of the wide range of articles and studies cited), which may well depart from the author's own suggestions or determinations.

One of the most charming features of the book is the creation of three fictional Irish poets with linguistically related names, each one representing a different time period and a related worldview. Each of these three fictional authors might have been familiar with the various 'worlds' of the Irish dreamtime, and would have been in a position to articulate them, in oral or literary form: *Katu-butos* (Iron Age, 300 BCE to 400 CE); *Cattubuttas* (Early Medieval period, 400-700 CE), and *Cathbad* (700-1000, the period during which the tales were set down on vellum). The concluding chapters of the study provide a variety of useful and thought-provoking assessments and interpretations of the extremely wide range of materials Mallory has addressed throughout the book. Lavishly illustrated with line drawings as well as colour and black-and-white photographs, *In Search of the Irish Dreamtime* is an invaluable resource for exploring and understanding the mythic past described in the Irish origin legends.

Sharon Paice MacLeod

DOSSIER

THREE RESPONSES TO EMILY LYLE'S *TEN GODS*

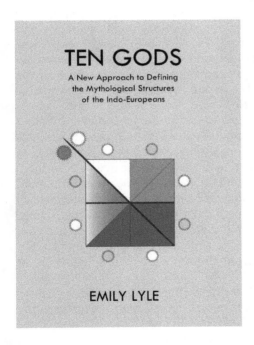

Ten Gods. A New Approach to Defining the Mythological Structures of the Indo-Europeans, by Emily Lyle. Newcastle-upon-Tyne: Cambridge Scholars Publishing, 2012. ISBN 978-1-4438-4156-6, £39.99, 155 pages.

RESPONSE 1

The last sentence of Lyle's book identifies the object of her work: "to articulate the proposed source of the scraps which, it is claimed, took the form to a well-crafted cosmology operating in terms of ten gods." As a scholar who has been much concerned with story-telling (in balladry, in Scotland and elsewhere) Lyle sets out to extricate a "story" from the Indo-European protomythic evidence: the aforementioned "scraps" or traces. Such "story" must have been first told before writing had reached the Indo-Europeans, and so depended on memory. Lyle's is a huge and complex task, possibly hubristic, and the culmination of decades of research and much thought, more thought, and rethinking.

Lyle obviously extends the analysis begun with Georges Dumézil's trifunctional theory, and already expanded by the Sauzeau brothers' "fourth function"[1] and the pentadic theory of Nick Allen (1986). The story she locates is revealed in Celtic, Germanic, Greek and Indic sources: a cosmological, inclusive, consistent account of origins and process. Her diagrams describe this big plan. The book's chapters are short, punchy, admirably concise and jargon-free. And she aims to convince us, while knowing that so large a project is vulnerable in its details, and open to attack on many varied fronts. How, to convince, for example, a German scholar who, when recently asked if he was going to hear a paper on the "fourth function," responded: "How can I believe in a 'fourth function' when I don't believe in the first three?" Perhaps it is not possible.

The core of Lyle's argument posits cosmic birth from a primal goddess (transmogrified into a giantess in the Germanic-Scandinavian context), from whom four generations of gods, human kings or divine 'creatures' (such as in the Irish Tuatha de Danann) descend. Macrocosmic world ages, the microcosmic human drama of ageing, the daily circuit of the sun, the monthly career of the moon, as well as the seasonal cycle, illustrate and reinforce this central myth. Other thematic stories ("recovery of the young goddess" and "castration and birth," for example) can be slotted into the conceived structure.

I am convinced that no reader would feel his or her time is wasted on delving into these usually translucent chapters, with their wealth of perceptions, webs of conclusions – and withal an array of provocations – but the question remains: how should this theory (or collection of theories, or narrative) be received and used? Lyle wants it to be used. She has made her own path clear, creating this book as a culmination of several decades of published articles (as the Sauzeau brothers did and Nick Allen has not, at least to date – though I am not criticizing Allen).

Is the cast of characters too large, the categories and images too diffuse? Ten gods are a lot of gods, even organized as Lyle sees them in the various narratives. I admit to using Dumézil's trifunctional system simply because it works, especially in parsing royal ritual (for instance, in the Byzantine context, or in medieval Europe, where scholars such as Joël Grisward and Patrice LaJoye also have delved with Dumézil's tools, and found gold). Allen's ideas on comparative myth have great merit and utility in certain contexts, and so does the quadratic system of the Sauzeau brothers, with the emphasis on "alterity and marginality." No emendation of Dumézil so far has ever completely eliminated or cast out his trifunctional mythographic scheme – and his original creative methods and insights are visible here in Lyle, as well they must be.

Recognizing both stimulus and goal, and as an initial critique as well, I think that there are gaps and lacunae in Lyle's narrative that need to be filled; and, with luck, they will be. Colour symbolism can be tricky and misleading, even when the symbolic values are agreed upon (I myself am inclined to privilege gray: a no-colour with sinister subtones – the colour assigned to a smithed weapon, or a wolf). The female gender is still underused here (virgins, vengeful widows, old women imaged as men?). The old king/young king (or old god and young god) in opposition, as in Saxo's story of the flawed hero Starcatherus/Starkaðr. And so on – I transcribe here marginal notes.

I must add that Lyle's bibliography displays her remarkable breadth of scholarship, and is especially valuable in that it stresses recent research and thinking on a very wide range of topics.

It would be most regrettable for Lyle's *Ten Gods* to be pecked to death, or die the death of a thousand cuts: it deserves a better fate. This is a serious book which rewards serious scrutiny – a most honourable entry in the field of grand narrative reconstruction: the study and explication of the Indo-European collectivity of stories, 'remembered' in hundreds of variants, but massively fragmented, after all the millennia.

Dean A. Miller

Notes

1   Lyle's bibliography includes an early sketch by the Sauzeaus, but their 2012 book clearly appeared too late to be included.

References

Allen, Nick J. 1986. "Tetradic Theory: An Approach to Kinship." *Journal of the Anthropological Society of Oxford* 17:87-109.

Sauzeau, Pierre and André Sauzeau. 2012. *La quatrième fonction. Alterité et marginalité dans l'idéologie des Indo-Européens.* Paris: Les Belle Lettres.

RESPONSE 2

In the title of Emily Lyle's newest book there are two notions that arouse interest at first glance: "ten gods" and "a new approach." What new approach could justify such a big number of gods and why exactly this number? How does it enrich the research of Indo-European cosmology?

The author's motivation and goal, best defined in the introduction and last chapter, point to a definite confidence in the fulfilled task. Presenting her argument through a linguistic metaphor, as the "grammar" of the myths which consists of ten "cases" / ten gods, Lyle (115) describes her motivation: the sense that a great gap existed in our knowledge, that could only be filled with a fresh orientation.

The author comments that, as is the case also in linguistics, diachronic changes definitely must be an object of research. Before that, however, the state before changes must be taken into consideration: the integrated Proto-Indo-European cosmology before literacy. The new approach, the author stresses, treats the myths themselves as embodied stories that had a life in relation to the society in which they were conceived. It was so long ago that linguistic comparison cannot immediately reach it (1). With her "grammar" of myths, Lyle points to the strong correspondence of human and divine sequences in the Indo-European context. The author finds the "capsule," the independent and separated unit, the time block of four generations both by humans and gods.

Building upon George Dumézil's structuralist comparative research into Indo-European nations' myths and religions, Lyle abandons his triple model (although she relies on it), and introduces a new one consisting of ten gods. She offers a theoretical construct in which these ten gods reflect human organizations in the earliest ages. They are all positioned into a net of relations they had within social reality and the symbolic constructs of time and space crucial for specific communities.

The book consists of ten chapters in 155 pages. This is not a large number of pages, but reading them is not easy; it requires great dedication and concentration. Each chapter builds on the previous one and requires the accumulated necessary contextual knowledge.

The first chapter is dedicated to the topic of memory storage without writing, the importance of the accumulation, retention and oral transmission of knowledge, with all the capabilities as well as the limitations of this method. The emergence of a structured cosmology is argued to be part of that same cognitive need.

Social structures in age-grade systems and in social institutions are dealt with in the second and third chapters. Continuing from Kim McCone's contribution, which replaced Dumézil's triple model of social classes of priests, warriors and cultivators, Lyle offers a new, complex and theoretically abstract model, placing the gods in the genealogical framework of a human royal family. To strengthen her thesis, she also uses ethnological comparisons with contemporary traditional cultures.

In the fourth chapter, "The Four-Generation Capsule and Royal Succession," the author clearly illustrates her thesis. By precisely drawing a graphical demonstration of the genealogical tree through four generations, Lyle places on the royal (and, by the same token, divine) hereditary 'throne' the ten principal persons from the royal house who correspond to the ten gods – from the young king to his great-great-grandmother. In Indo-European cosmogony, there is a story about three generations of kings originating from a primal goddess. Like human beings, the gods have their own personal identities, each has his own place in the genealogical sequence, each is labelled either as a king or through their relation to him.

"The World Ages and the Spatiotemporal Places of the Gods" is the title of the fifth chapter, which discusses the mythological spatiotemporal aspect. Each god has a place in the spatiotemporal sequence in which two separated places for kings exist, as well as eight identical non-royal niches. Lyle compares the historical periods of cosmic time with the parts of the human life cycle, using Arnold Gennep's Rites of Passage.

In the chapters that follow before the concluding and consolidating tenth chapter, the author discusses concrete gods in the Celtic (chapter 6), Germanic (chapter 7), Indian (chapter 8) and Greek (chapter 9) pantheons. However, in the sixth chapter dedicated to the Celts, Lyle gives a presentation of her own method which she calls the 'analogical' 'discovery method' (59). She abandons the former 'argument by analogy' introducing the 'discovery through' analogy, in a way in which we are more accustomed for the natural than the humanistic sciences.

Taking into account the island and not continental Celts, in this chapter the author speaks about the mythological birth of the primal goddess and stresses the adequacy of the term 'matrifocality'. She does this on the basis of the importance of women in mythological narratives (justifiably avoiding the notion of 'matriarchy'). In the context of the Germanic pantheon in particular, she speaks about the death of the god Baldr. From the Indian epic narratives, she picks out the motive of the young woman/ goddess.

In the Greek pantheon (chapter 9) special attention is dedicated to the connection of castration and birth (i.e. Hesiod's story about Aphrodite born from genitals thrown into the sea). Lyle compares this motive with similar ones from the Baltic East, India and Japan. Calling upon Mircea Eliade, Lyle speaks about the primal goddess as the container of unborn gods (connecting the river Tigris and the releasing of waters with the birth of young gods). At the same time, the author uses the same metaphor (container) when speaking generally about the myths as the containers of a 'generative grammar' of (Indo-European) culture. The author connects the narrative about birth with the releasing of waters from the rivers which have their spring in the procreative organ of the Great Goddess.

One part of the ninth chapter particularly stands out: birth connected with another cosmic topic – the hero who releases the waters by defeating the dragon. In a recent article Lyle (2015) expanded on this topic, identifying the dragon with the goddess Earth. In this article, but not in the book, the author also discusses the Croatian scholar Radoslav Katičić's research about the golden key, which in Slavic mythology opens the earth in Spring, and about St. George who, by beheading the dragon, opens the fertile period of the year.

This book definitely does not leave the reader indifferent. On the contrary, by its intriguing nature, it makes us ponder and rethink already adopted views. By its revolutionary postulates – not only because it abandons the tripartite model of Indo-European mythic structure – the book sometimes induces disbelief and reconsideration. It inverts settled notions, such as the notion of matrilineal inheritance as a (pre-Indo-European) layer before its collision with a patrilineal way of organising inheritance, supposed to have been imposed after the Indo-European penetration (Lyle admonishes that cosmology does not support such an invasive scenario).

The author gives us a more homogenous picture of gods and goddesses, thus shaking up the present understanding about the Indo-Europeans. She specifically stresses that her investigations show that goddesses played a central, though not dominant, role within the pantheon in prehistory (115). There is no doubt that Emily Lyle's scientific endeavour can be qualified as highly professional, innovative and also brave. It will certainly foster academic debate, and become an important spring board for further investigations of comparative Indo-European mythology.

Jelka Vince Pallua

References

Lyle, Emily. 2015. "The Hero Who Releases the Waters and Defeats the Flood Dragon." *Comparative Mythology* 1:1-12.

RESPONSE 3

The challenge of mythology, as Claude Lévi-Strauss once observed, is that "in a myth anything is likely to happen [but] this apparent arbitrariness is belied by the astounding similarity between myths collected in different regions" (Lévi-Strauss 1955, 429). In other words, myth presents its audience with a semi-structured system, which simultaneously invites and refuses reduction to a simpler model. The cognitive perils of such systems are well-known. By displaying principles of order that are too weak to be properly regarded as laws, they grant the interpretive consciousness the freedom to discover correlations without the corrective of falsification that has proved so valuable in the exact sciences. Too often — as evinced by the history of comparative mythology — this has resulted in subjectivism run riot, where mythology becomes a machinery for reproducing the intuitions of its analyst.

It is to Emily Lyle's immense credit that, in *Ten Gods*, she so successfully treads the fine line between confirmation bias and informed judgment. In reconstructing the Indo-European pantheon, Lyle builds on a body of work familiar to anyone who has worked in the area of comparative mythology—most obviously her monograph *Archaic Cosmos* (1990), but also a small library's worth of articles that chart the taxonomical decisions of Indo-European thought. As with her previous expositions, Lyle's current offering combines both incision and provocation. The incision lies in her ability to cut straight to the essential materials of her thesis (and the relevant secondary literature); the provocation derives from her model's capacity to stimulate independent development in the reader.

The core claim of Lyle's system is relatively straightforward. For her, the primordial Indo-European creation myth charts a process of generation, in which an original goddess births one god with whom she copulates to produce two sons. A further round of copulation with these three fathers produces five further gods and a goddess, with a king of the gods and a counter-king among the five new gods. The end result is a pantheon of ten gods, who emerge across a three-generational cycle and are united by common ancestry.

On their own, reconstructions of this sort are merely diverting; to stimulate real interest they need to solve problems. Happily, Lyle's theory does exactly this. In a display of immense erudition, she traces how the purported pantheon manifests itself in the mythological narratives, cosmological structures and kinship models of various Indo-European cultures. Her proposal is that the ten gods, appropriately grouped by category (two goddesses, king and counter-king, etc.), define mutually reinforcing mnemonic and spatiotemporal systems. Mnemonic, because the groupings correspond to the 7±2 items constraint on working memory; spatiotemporal, because the groupings align with the eight locations in an oriented three-dimensional space. The connection derives from value of spatial systems for encoding memories. Given the challenges of recording information in preliterate cultures, this meant that, for any society that "placed a high value on the accumulation, retention and transmission of knowledge, the creation of a structured cosmology was a cognitive necessity" (9).

It would do little justice to the richness of Lyle's book to offer potted summaries of the various instances in which she uses her system to good effect. Suffice to say that she leavens studies of social institutions like age grade systems, kingship, mythic cosmology and succession with an appreciation of cultural variation in Celtic, Germanic, Indian and Classical materials. A more useful procedure is to show how she performs one comparative exercise — the study of the birth narratives of Zeus and the Irish hero-god, Lugaid of the Red Stripes, in Chapter 6. Lyle's goal here is to use analogical correlation "to disclose patterns of myth that may lie behind the narratives" (59), with her reconstructed pantheon providing the latent pattern.

Citing Gilles Fauconnier's theory of conceptual blends, Lyle proceeds by claiming that the accounts of Zeus's birth in Hesiod and Lugaid's in the *Dindsenchas* can be thought of as input spaces in a conceptual blend, with the latter abstracting the common structure from both narratives. The common structure derives from the fact that both Zeus and Lug are kings marked by an association with three males and one female—through descent in Zeus's case (Gaia, Uranus, Cronos, Poseidon), and by way of sibling affiliation in Lugaid's (Clothru, Nár, Lothar, Bres). However, this blended space can in turn function as an input space in a further round of correlation, and do so iteratively. This allows Lyle to bring in Welsh (Lleu) and Egyptian (Horus) materials that add a counter-king (the king of the dead) to the taxonomy. As such, her method allows her to sieve through the various mythological traditions in way that retains the essential correspondences while dispensing with incidental details. One result is to offer a far more nuanced appreciation of the Celtic pantheon than that offered by (say) Dumézil's trifunctionalism, which unduly constrains how different personages can be grouped together. Another is to disclose hitherto unguessed at links between diverse stories that point to their common origin in the cognitive models of prehistory. In all cases, Lyle's approach leads to an increase in our knowledge of mythological materials.

Viewing matters from a more general perspective, a particular achievement of Lyle's method is to show up the need to complement the analysis of mythological narratives with an appreciation of anthropological context. Having been out of fashion for some time, phylogenetic approaches to culture are currently enjoying a renaissance, driven mostly by developments in statistics and computer analysis (Atkinson and Whitehouse 2011; Graça, Tehrani and Graça 2016; Ross, Greenhill and Atkinson 2013; Stubbersfield, Tehrani and Flynn 2014; Tehrani 2013). Unfortunately, sophisticated methods do not always produce sophisticated results, and the conclusions reached are presented without any real understanding of how ecological, social and cognitive factors shape and re-shape narrative materials — typically, by way of inversions and displacements that cannot be accounted for by similarity-based modelling. *Ten Gods* reminds us that mythology does not occur in a vacuum, and any real appreciation of how it functions can only be obtained by a patient, diligent immersion in the history of peoples and social institutions.

If there are few weaknesses in Lyle's work, one of them must be the absence (one could almost say the phobic absence) of a reflection on the work of Lévi-Strauss. To be sure, it is not mandated that one must discuss Lévi-Strauss; indeed, there is an argument to be made that his influence on comparative mythological studies remains so pervasive that space should be made for other approaches. Nevertheless, the fact is that aspects of Lyle's system would profit from being juxtaposed against Lévi-Strauss's work. This is obviously the case where they align with each other: the iterative process of conceptual blending that Lyle proposes on Chapter 6, for example, is not unlike the account of mythic dialectics outlined by Lévi-Strauss in "The Structural Study of Myth" (1955), while the combinatorial system underlying the spatiotemporal, kinship and royal succession models in *Ten Gods* invites comparison with similar operations in "The Story of Asdiwal" (1967). However, it is where the approaches diverge that one would most like to see the encounter occur. Lévi-Strauss, famously, rejected the programme of phylogenetic reconstruction with the claim that the structural method "eliminates a problem which has so far been one of the main obstacles to the progress of mythological studies, namely, the quest for the *true* version, or the *earlier* one" (Lévi-Strauss, 1955, 435). It is hard to imagine that a scholar as accomplished as Lyle is unfamiliar with this claim and the challenge it poses to her method, and her disinclination to engage directly with it is a puzzling lapse.

This issue notwithstanding, *Ten Gods* remains a vital contribution to the field of comparative methodology. Whether by the force of its conclusions or the innovations of its methods, it shows how ingenuity can cast new light on cultural materials that have been with us since prehistory. The project initiated by this book is far from finished; one hopes to see more rewards follow from it in the near future.

James Carney

References

Atkinson, Q. D. and H. Whitehouse. 2011. "The cultural morphospace of ritual form. Examining modes of religiosity cross-culturally." *Evolution and Human Behavior* 32 (1): 50–62. doi:10.1016/j.evolhumbehav.2010.09.002.

Graça, S., J.J. Tehrani and S. Graça, S. 2016. "Comparative phylogenetic analyses uncover the ancient roots of Indo-European folktales." *Royal Society Open Science* 3:1–11.

Lévi-Strauss, C. 1955. "The Structural Study of Myth." *The Journal of American Folklore* 68 (270): 428–444.

Lévi-Strauss, C. 1967. "The Story of Asdiwal." In *The Structural Study of Myth and Totemism*, edited by E. Leach, 1–48. London: Tavistock Publications.

Lyle, E. 1990. *Archaic Cosmos: Polarity, Space and Time*. Edinburgh: Polygon.

Ross, R. M., S. J. Greenhill and Q.D. Atkinson. 2013. "Population structure and cultural geography of a folktale in Europe." In *Proceedings of the Royal Society* B, 280, 20123065. doi:10.1098/rspb.2012.3065

Stubbersfield, J. M., J. J. Tehrani and E. G. Flynn. 2014. "Serial killers, spiders and cybersex: Social and survival information bias in the transmission of urban legends." *British Journal of Psychology*: 1–20. doi:10.1111/bjop.12073

Tehrani, J. J. 2013. "The phylogeny of Little Red Riding Hood." *PLOS ONE* 8 (11):np. doi:10.1371/journal.pone.0078871

CPSIA information can be obtained
at www.ICGtesting.com
Printed in the USA
BVHW081843061118
532329BV00011B/131/P